BOOKS WITH MEN BEHIND THEM

BOOKS BY EDMUND FULLER

A Pageant of the Theatre
John Milton
A Star Pointed North (*novel*)
Brothers Divided (*novel*)
George Bernard Shaw: Critic of Western Morale
Vermont: A History of the Green Mountain State
Tinkers and Genius:
The Story of the Yankee Inventors
Man in Modern Fiction
Books with Men Behind Them

BOOKS
WITH MEN
BEHIND THEM

by

EDMUND FULLER

RANDOM HOUSE · NEW YORK

12/1962
Gen.

For Faith

Acknowledgments

The author wishes to thank the following publishers and agents for permission to quote from their books:

Albert and Charles Boni, Inc., for *The Bridge of San Luis Rey, The Cabala, The Woman of Andros,* by Thornton Wilder; Cambridge University Press for *An Experiment in Criticism,* by C. S. Lewis, and *The Two Cultures,* by C. P. Snow; The Dial Press, Inc., for Gladys Schmitt: *The Gates of Aulis* (Copyright 1942 by Gladys Schmitt), *David the King* (Copyright 1946 by Gladys Schmitt), *Alexandra* (Copyright 1947 by Gladys Schmitt), *Confessors of the Name* (Copyright 1952 by Gladys Schmitt), *A Small Fire* (Copyright © 1957 by Gladys Schmitt); Grove Press, Inc., for *Tropic of Cancer,* by Henry Miller (Copyright © 1961 by Grove Press, Inc.); Harcourt, Brace & World, Inc., for *Surprised by Joy* and *The World's Last Night,* by C. S. Lewis; Harper & Brothers for *Our Town, The Ides of March, The Matchmaker, The Skin of Our Teeth, Heaven's My Destination,* by Thornton Wilder; Harvard University Press for

Science and Government, by C. P. Snow; Houghton Mifflin Company for *The Hobbit* and *The Lord of the Rings,* by J. R. R. Tolkien; The Macmillan Company and Geoffrey Bles Ltd. for *The Screwtape Letters* and *The Voyage of the Dawn Treader,* by C. S. Lewis; Oxford University Press for essays by C. S. Lewis and J. R. R. Tolkien in *Essays Presented to Charles Williams* and for *Charles Williams: Selected Writings;* Random House, Inc., for *Rembrandt,* by Gladys Schmitt (Copyright © 1961 by Gladys Schmitt); Charles Scribner's Sons for *The Children of the Night,* by Edwin Arlington Robinson; Charles Scribner's Sons and Jonathan Cape Limited for *Cry, the Beloved Country* and *Too Late the Phalarope,* by Alan Paton; Charles Scribner's Sons and Macmillan & Co. Ltd. (London) for *The Affair, The Conscience of the Rich, The Light and the Dark, The Masters, The New Men, Time of Hope, Strangers and Brothers,* by C. P. Snow; A. Watkins, Inc., for Charles Williams: *The Place of the Lion* (© 1951 Pellegrini & Cudahy), *The Greater Trumps* (© 1950 Pellegrini & Cudahy), *Many Dimensions* (© 1949 Pellegrini & Cudahy), *Shadows of Ecstasy* (© 1950 Pellegrini & Cudahy), *All Hallows' Eve* (© 1948 Pellegrini & Cudahy), *War in Heaven* (© 1949 Pellegrini & Cudahy), *Descent into Hell* (© 1949 Pellegrini & Cudahy).

Contents

BOOKS WITH MEN BEHIND THEM

Books with men behind them

Emerson said, "Talent alone cannot make a writer. There must be a man behind the book." What should be self-evident has become a striking notion in this age of mass publication. Nowadays we tend to reverse the idea and accept somewhat indiscriminately as a writer any man with books behind him.

The man behind the book, which I take as the unifying concept to link together the discussions in these pages, clearly is required to have something more than talent. One of the troubles of a glibly articulate time is that talent is extolled by itself, and sometimes no other qualifying appraisal is made. Many a wretched book has been foisted upon us on the dubious plea that the writer had talent.

I must define my terms—both *talent* and *man*—in the present context. Certain definitions from the *Oxford English Dictionary* support my view of talent: "Mental endowment; natural ablity . . . Aptitudes or faculties of various kinds . . . Mental power or ability; cleverness." Applied to writers, in these terms, talent should be taken for granted as the minimal technical equipment necessary to get into print. It should never have to be remarked in any critical discussion. No one would begin a review of a violinist's concert debut by commending him for being able to play. Professionalism assumed, in any art, one then begins to approach the judgment of essential merit: exceptional refinements of craft, individuality, interpretation, or content, as appropriate to the medium.

It is easy to make too much of the mere fact that a man can write: that he has some articulateness, some mastery of narrative, exposition, imagery or invention. The ability to command such rhetorical skills in their basic forms is relatively commonplace among us. It is seen in people of sensitivity, integrity and wisdom. It is also found in knaves, fools, the irresponsible and, most subtle difficulty of all, those who have nothing worth saying with it. Talent is the equipment that may make achievement possible. Achievement is what it is our business to judge. In the art of writing, this appraisal brings us right up against the man. In noting the existence of literary talent the man is not taken into account; in weighing literary achievement we will find a figure of consequence behind work of consequence. Inconsequential, irresponsible, or immature work lacks the man behind it.

This should not evoke a cry of protest against *ad hominem* criticism. Clearly we do not measure the work by the man's private, extra-literary personality or actions. The man *behind* the book, in Emerson's sense, is in fact *in* the book: not necessarily in his own proper person, not necessarily in the forefront, but nonetheless within its frame. No probing criticism of either a body of work or a single volume can fail to uncover the man.

What is this *man?* In the sense of my text it is not simply that lumpen forked figure of genus Homo, per se; nor is it a question of gender. The *Oxford English Dictionary* offers under the heading "Man" five large three-column pages. I am using the word, as clearly Emerson was, to distinguish the best, in the spirit of Antony's tribute to the dead Brutus: "this was a man." To turn to Emerson again, he described the scholar as "man thinking." In such terms we might consider the artist as "man thinking and feeling." In both cases, the conscious formalization of the process and the deliberate, productive doing something about it, are assumed. Justice Holmes defended his severely intellectual approach to the law by insisting, "To think is not less than to feel." Artists tacitly operate on the premise that to feel is not less than to think. The greatest artists always have done both.

A man, then, is one who has ripened some ordered, rational and balanced vision of life and of the nature of his kind. His work should not be considered just the container of his vision, it *is* the vision. The mature artist will not presume to encompass, define (or confine) truth, yet he will be concerned with the truth of what he says. He will not carelessly confuse *truth* with what is called *reality*, for though these two are intimately related, not every reality, by itself, constitutes a truth, for truths lie in complex patterns of realities. The ultimate truth is equated with total reality and is not accessible to anyone but God.

There are many truths (love, for instance—love of any kind—is one such) that cannot be tested in the laboratory sense as realities. Nor will the artist confuse honesty with truth, for though they, too, are related, the world is full of honest error and ignorance. Nor, beyond modest limits, will he confuse either self-awareness or a candid reporting of experience with truth. Both of these may be desirable things, good in themselves and contributing to truth, yet the solipsistic insistence that private experience and individual self-awareness are the only truths is a blight upon much contemporary thought and literature.

If the writer builds his structure on any of these fragments to the exclusion of all else; or if, as is all too common, he writes blindly, emotionally, in muddled and inconsistent images of life, there is not a man behind his book. Behind many of the novels and plays of our time there are only weeping, frightened, fretful or rebellious children—or occasionally, maimed men. This fact, and the kinds of success that they often achieve, alike are symptoms of the dis-ordered age, haunted by sensuality and violence in the wake and threat of war, with many frightened to hysteria by the shadow of the bomb. Never has the puerile, the immature, the adolescent (actual or perennial) had such acceptance, or been listened to almost as a sage. The adolescent is bad enough as the dictator of popular arts, taste, conduct and mer-chandising; as a literary arbiter he is intolerable.

The man behind a work may be of many sorts or hold many views, and I do not attempt to confine him to any profession of faith or orthodoxy. But two things are minimal requirements for the present defi-nition: a conviction of the essential dignity of the creature, however flawed and divided, and a belief in the inherent meaningfulness not just of human life but of all creation.

In *Man in Modern Fiction*, in 1958, I discussed many books that have no men behind them, as well as a few that do. Since the chief preoccupation of that book was the discussion of how the image of man has been distorted in modern writing, and since the demonstration of that involved a great deal of con-temporary writing that I do not admire, it was pri-marily a book of attack.

I am not trying to prevent, or even discourage, the reading of any books I don't like. I am merely say-ing what I think about them. On the other hand, I am actively interested in promoting the reading of books I admire. So in this volume I take a particular pleasure in praising a group of writers. There should be no richer satisfaction for the critic when it is possible. Except for the chapter called "The Post-Chatterley Deluge," which examines some developments since the earlier book and thus serves to link the two, praise is the dominant tone of this volume. It is truly a companion to *Man in Modern Fiction* in that it has the same preoccupation with the image of man, but is chiefly exploring that image in the work of a number of writers, of widely differing characteristics, who have in common a balanced, comprehensive, realistic, authentically compassionate and mature vision of man.

The restoration or rehabilitation of man is immensely important in our contemporary literature. Man cannot muster his resources to rise to the crisis of survival in the nuclear age if he does not conceive himself to be a creature worth saving, or with the capacity to help himself, or with sources of strength outside and above himself. This is certainly a time when, in Melville's words, in *Moby Dick*,

> Men may seem detestable as joint stock-companies and nations; knaves, fools, and murderers there may be; men may have mean and meagre faces; but man, in the ideal, is so noble and so sparkling, such a grand and glowing creature, that over any ignominious blemish in him all his fellows should run to throw their costliest robes.

All tendencies need balancing correctives, including the one articulated there by Melville and amply balanced in the same work, but a dose of that spirit is sorely needed in our time, in and out of books.

The quiet but powerful countercurrent toward a sound vision of man, which I remarked among younger writers, continues to flow, even under the surface turbulence of the post-Chatterley deluge. Certain well-remembered books of the last few years typify it, but by no means exhaust it. John Hersey—scarcely a newcomer—continued his concerned and humane examination of modern problems, and his experiments with form, in *The Child Buyer*.

A book to stir the conscience of the world, deep in its humanity, came from abroad, where, as here, it reached a huge audience: *The Last of the Just*, by André Schwarz-Bart—another demonstration that the image of man can be upheld in the midst of the most appalling indictment of the crimes of man.

In *Set This House on Fire*, a book longer than it needed to be, and carrying some of its elements to excesses in the mode of the time, William Styron revealed a major step in the maturing of his considerable powers. It carried some of the hip behavior patterns to their logical conclusions with a power that at once set him apart from and beyond the Mailer-Jones school of writing with which he had often been bracketed. It won him increased respect in many quarters, but a few of those who had praised him highly before, turned on him for daring to move out of the category where they thought they had him pegged. If the direction Styron has taken in this book is sustained, it promises much.

Morris West's *The Devil's Advocate*, Giuseppi di Lampedusa's posthumous *The Leopard*, and John Knowles's *A Separate Peace* graced their seasons.

Two books, both first novels, had a particular impact upon many. Eugene Vale's *The Thirteenth Apostle* was an ambitious allegorical structure, bold in reach and conception and eloquent in execution. It received much acclaim and caused reviewers, in appraising it, to cast about for such names as Mann, Camus, and Bunyan; the first two because of its probing, brooding modern intellectual quest, the latter because it is a type of Pilgrim's Progress of our time in its spiritual search. It deals also with the pursuit of a soul by God, as in "The Hound of Heaven." An American consul in a small Central American country is called into the interior in search of information about the death of an artist. He finds himself, to his terror and distress, caught in an investigation that touches the deepest caverns of his own being and draws him irresistibly to the ascent of a great mountain in pursuit of the enigma. The book has probing things to say about art, as well as about the nature of man and the mysteries of his relations with God. It has been published in England and Europe and is, I think, certain to be read for a long time.

The second of the two failed to receive a general recognition commensurate with its merit, partly because of the resistance of some people to serious consideration of anything that is identified as science fiction. Yet upon many, including such a discerning critic as R. W. B. Lewis, it made a strong impact. This was *A Canticle for Leibowitz*, by Walter M. Miller, Jr. Like Nevil Shute's *On the Beach* it deals with the aftermath of an atomic holocaust, but there resemblance ceases. Shute's interesting book was stoically defeatist and shallow in its philosophy.

Miller employs a bold structure. His book carries us into the future in three great strides. He shows us the gradual recovery of man and of civilization in periods analogous to the Dark Ages, the Renaissance, and the modern scientific era, only to plunge us once more into the abyss. He is illuminating our present and possible future by our past, and is also renewing our understanding of what that past has been. It is grim, but not despairing; he does not obliterate the species, like Shute, but in several subtle ways works in terms of that great biblical concept, "the remnant." The book is at once terrifying and exhilarating. Miller has keen wit and good scholarship, in addition to his storyteller's art; the fruit is a book extraordinarily imaginative and fresh, that manages to be both funny and appalling, at appropriate times, with no clash of these qualities. It is an experience not to be missed and offers the deepest fictional reflections on the implications of an apocalyptic age that I have seen anywhere.

Different in its nature, but also impressive, was a first novel, *The Important Thing*, by Robert Granat.

It received none of the attention it deserved, partly perhaps because it was a war book, late in the stream of its genre. It was unusual among combat books in the maturity of its vision of a man struggling desperately to be human, in both war and peace. Certain scenes were as fine and memorable as anything in recent writing. This novel and other shorter things of Granat's that have appeared in *New World Writing* and other media, mark him as a voice likely to be heard further and rewardingly.

The men—and one woman—whose work I discuss at length in the ensuing chapters do not represent any school or homogeneous group, although the total body of work of each one of them richly exemplifies my theme of books with men behind them. They are not offered as a cross-section of the modern literary scene here or abroad. They represent a few writers of diverse sorts whom I admire for a variety of qualities, and about whom I felt I had something to say that others have not said. This last consideration accounts for the omission of a number of major writers—perhaps most notably William Faulkner—for whom I have deep admiration but whose work has generated a vast body of critical discussion, sound and otherwise, which I have no present wish to join.

In the work of the writers praised here, the reaffirmation of man in modern fiction is seen in many different facets, overlapping and harmonizing. We find explorations of power ranging from political and economic power in the work of the humanist, Snow, to supernatural power in the work of the Christian mystic, Williams. Wilder also touches the theme in his portrait of Caesar; and Gladys Schmitt, in her studies of Saul and David, and of the third-century Roman Emperor Decius. Tolkien evokes the sinister aspects of power in terms of fantasy. C. S. Lewis touches it in the vein of science fiction in *That Hideous Strength,* and it is interesting to consider his "National Institute for Co-ordinated Experiments" beside Snow's "new men." In Alan Paton, we see the effects of power wielded by a dominant state and race.

Paton affords us also some interesting reflections on the tragic and the question of whether Christianity lies beyond it, or whether Christian man may be used as a figure of tragedy. There is a sense in which the Christian vision can be the basis for the deepest tragedy, yet one susceptible of redemption. The element of stature needed for the tragic figure is supplied by the vision of men as responsible creatures of God, capable of becoming sons of God. There is no greater fall, after the angels, than that of man in the Judeo-Christian myth. Where man is conscious of what he is and what he was meant to be, and acts in that consciousness, we may have that tragic blend of grandeur and misery that is so fascinating in his greatest art and his highest moments in history.

In Gladys Schmitt and in Wilder we have much conscious meditation on the nature and problems of the artist (as also in Vale's *The Thirteenth Apostle*, mentioned above). Charles Williams touches this somewhat, also, in the poet Stanhope, in *Descent into Hell*, and more cursorily, in the painter, Drayton, in *All Hallows' Eve*.

In another parallel, Gladys Schmitt's third-century Roman patrician, Favorinus, and Wilder's eighteenth-century Marquesa de Montemayor: neither of them can endure to live in a world with no plan or meaning. Also, these two writers in particular repeatedly show similar perceptions of the subtle, elusive nature of many modes of love.

A corollary to the debased image of man's nature is the cult of the abdication of reason, the disavowing of the mind, in much fiction. In all the writers here discussed, the powers and responsibilities of man's intellect have their full weight and respect. It might be noted that it takes a mind to cope with the mind.

In the writers that follow, their characters, from the homely to the extraordinary, from creator to destroyer, from believer to skeptic, from intuitive to intellectual, in love and hate and ambition and sacrifice, in exaltation and degradation, typify the procession of man—man who has been challenged and denied in much modern fiction, but not destroyed or lost. These writers are some among the many, and the more yet to come, who still comprehend the nature of man. In their work, too, we encounter at times the true strain of nobility: a commodity in short supply in modern writing. We need it both to feed the spirit and because of the polarization that requires the noble to make it possible to show the ignoble.

In the closing lines of his sonnet to George Crabbe, Edwin Arlington Robinson speaks of

> . . . the shame
> And emptiness of what our souls reveal
> In books that are as altars where we kneel
> To consecrate the flicker, not the flame.

In the books with men behind them, it is the flame we honor.

The post-Chatterley deluge

In his story of the day the dam broke, James Thurber described the people rushing through the streets crying, "Go east! Go east!" A dam of quite another kind has broken, but there seems to be no direction in which one can exhort people to go—unless perhaps up. We are caught in the flood of the post-Chatterley deluge.

In *Man in Modern Fiction*, in 1958, I remarked that "A man cannot get himself privately published any more . . . Even aging Henry Miller has found it impossible to remain beyond the pale. . . ." Sure enough, in keeping with the general acceleration of the age, first *Lady Chatterley's Lover* was with us, and then *Tropic of Cancer*, plus my real subject of concern, a lot of flotsam carried down the stream in their wake. Given the present American state of mind and the growing habit patterns of many of our writers, the torrent was inevitable and predictable.

Some minor ironies go with it. An American novelist, steadily becoming more publicized than productive, more read-about than read, was confidently at work on what he believed to be unpublishable material. In the first post-Chatterley rush, it was published without the faintest ripple of a shockwave, which may have shocked its author. He failed to produce either a censorship *cause célèbre* or a plain-wrapper package.

Since then, a withered under-the-counter classic, Henry Miller's *Tropic of Cancer*, has been trotted out by the same press that so selflessly gave us *Lady Chatterley*. Presumably cowed by the Chatterley experience, the postal department scarcely said a mumbling word. Thus a much more flagrant book, without even the solemnly befuddled integrity of Lawrence's, walked where that peculiar saint had trod, without challenge. *Tropic of Cancer's* desiccated reputation was resaturated with the juices of critical praise solicited from a variety of people whose sense of balance seemed destroyed entirely by the heady belief that they were opening new frontiers for art. Since then the way has been cleared for *Tropic of Capricorn* and the rest of the Miller canon.

I do not object to the publishing of any of these books and would be compelled, for the reasons set forth by Judge Bryan and Judge Woolsey, in their famous *Chatterley* and *Ulysses* decisions, to raise my voice against a move to ban them again. I am as much an enemy of censorship as the most ardent devotees of Lawrence or Miller. But I do deplore the flood of fatuous comment brought forth about those books from generally reputable literary people. I do see problems involved in the consequences of this freedom, the first of which is the general denial that there is any problem.

Once the Chatterley case had been won, it was clear within the next publishing season that a wave of response had begun. This could be seen by any extensive reviewer of fiction, simply from the cross-section of books that came his way in routine assignment. It is this indiscriminate response that is of concern—not the Lawrence and Miller books.

Before this license, a Lawrence or Miller or Joyce had to have the unusual drive, peculiar conviction, and extra measure of talent to launch his work against the opposition of society-at-large. This was a guarantee that if such work found itself with an established reputation it had some substance and merit: these qualities ultimately find a general acceptance. This is a normal and appropriate history. The point is missed that *Ulysses* or *Lady Chatterley* or *Tropic of Cancer* probably would not have been written had there been no challenge implicit in writing them. I am protesting the consequences of the free invitation offered to any Tom, Dick or Harry to write with absolute license without the tests of proving themselves which made Joyce, Lawrence and Miller the men they are, for better or worse. The whole concept of *avant garde* vanishes if no price must be paid for a bold departure from a previous convention.

In the wake of the Chatterley case, writers decided, and editors concurred, that if not "anything goes" at least a great deal more would go than ever went before. A representative catalogue of titles to document this deluge would serve no purpose but to advertise some items that are already en route to oblivion, but in many books of serious literary pretensions (let alone the great number without such claims), new extremes of language, new minutiae of physical grapplings appeared, including details of homosexual encounters rivaling the scope of Lawrence's account of field days in the old-fashioned heterosexual game preserves. In a prominent journal one reviewer of the American edition of a Scandinavian novel marveled at things he had never seen in print before, but the palm for this distinction was quickly brought back from Scandinavia to the United States (along with the heavyweight boxing title), by one of the most touted books of the late 1959 season. It was clear that the wraps were off: new areas were open, and bigger exploitation of the old ones was in order.

Mail current with this writing brought a lavish brochure for a new, expensive, pseudo-intellectual-artistic fringe-type of magazine. It describes itself as "born as a result of the recent series of court decisions that have realistically interpreted America's obscenity laws and that have given to this country a

new breadth of freedom of expression. We refer to
the decisions which have enabled the publication of
such heretofore suppressed literary masterworks as
'Lady Chatterley's Lover.' " The publishers go on to
assure us of what was already evident, that the magazine "will take full advantage of this new freedom of
expression."

The ironies accumulate if we consider the cases of
the books that have loosed the flood on us. As for
Lady Chatterley, what was, in sober fact, gained for
the general weal by lifting the ban? The book is of
little real interest except to the close student of the
whole Lawrence canon. It was notoriously accessible
already to anyone who needed or desperately wanted
it. Every literary professional and most serious wide
readers were familiar with its unexpurgated version.
The largest group of people who did not previously
have ready access to it and now do, are teen-agers. It
is a ludicrously humorless, obsessive, true-believer's
book, a minor work in the author's total body, the
hullabaloo about which is more harmful than helpful to an understanding of Lawrence among any but
the best-informed readers. How infinitely regrettable
that innumerably more young minds may now meet
him as a weaver of flower garlands for the pubic
hair than as the author of *Sons and Lovers*. This result has been helped along by the absurdly out-of-
focus praises heaped upon it by prominent American
critics and writers. (Although many silly things
were said in the English trial, on the whole a more

balanced evaluation of the book and of its weak-
nesses and failures was developed, even from the
testimony of defense witnesses.)

On the other side, the dangerous absurdities of
censorship were innocently displayed by the post-
master general. He did his righteous best, with the
inevitable effect of strengthening the case against
censorship and adding to the circulation of what he
sought to suppress. The net result of the case was no
really significant freedom, nothing of major value
made available that hadn't been before, and no vin-
dication for Lawrence, who needed none. Rather,
the chief results were great profit for several publishers (who wrangled among themselves in the
courts over slices of the melon), the opening of
another general literary floodgate to the irresponsible, and the final elevation of *Lady Chatterley*, in a
mass-circulation paperback, to the possible status of
most widely bought, partially thumbed through, and
least fully read book in history. What would Lawrence (who could have used some of the money)
have thought about that?

Tropic of Cancer is another matter. It lacks the
peculiar moral intention of Lawrence. It is a nihilistic,
anarchistic book, equally dated in many ways. Now,
when this generation's counterparts of the younger
Henry Miller display a frantic anxiety lest the world
be blown up, and some cite the H-bomb in justifica-
tion of their protest behavior, it is odd to read Miller
saying: "The world is rotting away, dying piece-

meal. But it needs the *coup de grâce*, it needs to be blown to smithereens."

The essence of the philosophy of *Tropic of Cancer* is, "I want the whole world to be out of whack, I want everyone to scratch himself to death." Another revealing line, sounding like an earlier but more genuinely talented Kerouac: "I have moved the typewriter into the next room where I can see myself in the mirror as I write."

Tropic of Cancer is, in truth, a cancerous book with the thrust of a vivid personality and flashes of the Rabelaisian comic spirit. It paints memorable scenes of Paris. It has good and bad things in it. It would be silly to suppose, in quite another use of the words, that it would be all "good" if the "bad" things were taken out of it. That is not the problem of the book at all. The problem is its vision of life and man and its conception of art. It is a sick man's idea of a healthy book. Some of its proponents praise it as ferociously moral. It rejects some things that deserve rejection, but if blind rebellion and indiscriminate striking out against all the standards of society are to be accepted as a moral indictment, with unabashed personal irresponsibility and nothing offered in place of what is rejected, then and only then can *Tropic of Cancer* be called other than a "bad boy's" exhibitionism.

It is a more barbaric yawp than Whitman ever dreamt of raising. Miller adheres to his own dictum: "Art consists in going the full length. If you start with the drums you have to end with dynamite, or TNT." (This is the dilemma of most of our supposedly bold or tough writers.) As a nay-sayer to all society and all standards, interpreting the various sins of all as the total hypocrisy of all, he is touted by admirers as a true moralist. Miller is amoral. Like the mule butting into the tree, he isn't blind, he just doesn't give a damn. He is irresponsible in the profoundest meaning of the word. He is the man Khrushchev says doesn't exist:

> I haven't any allegiances, any responsibilities, any hatreds, any worries, any prejudices, any passion. I'm neither for nor against. I'm a neutral.

Like so many others who are mispraised for vitality when they are actually life-denying, he insists upon "the hideousness of reality" and he sees the prime motive of any action or idea as the futile attempt to "render life tolerable," for "the greater part of what happens is just muck and filth, sordid as any garbage can. . . ." When Swift said much the same thing he set over against the Yahoo element in mankind the noble image of the Houyhnhnms as a model for reform. Miller has no such interest, there is no counterbalancing vision. He is content with his observation:

> No matter where you go, no matter what you touch, there is cancer and syphilis. It is written in the sky, it flames and dances like an evil portent. It has eaten into our souls and we are nothing but a dead thing like the moon.

Now his scabrous and colorful work is snatched from the under-counter booksellers, whose stock-in-trade he has been for years. But it is not just offered for sale openly. It is elevated. Karl Shapiro, in a hysterically fulsome introduction, calls him "the greatest living author . . . Miller's achievement is miraculous. . . ." Horace Gregory calls the book "Huck Finn in Paris" (Maurice Dolbier waggishly suggests it might be a misprint), a totally inept analogy except as it points to Miller himself as a romantic "bad boy" image. Harry T. Moore attributes to it "the innocence of the unself-conscious." The mirror quotation above, by itself should dispose of the notion of unself-consciousness. Norman Cousins congratulates the publishers on "courage and good taste," which, whatever else may be said, is as odd a choice of encomiums to apply to this case as could be dredged up anywhere. Sir Herbert Read solemnly proclaims it, "One of the most significant contributions to the literature of our times," which, standing alone, is about as cryptic as you can get. And at last, John Ciardi, a translator of Dante, assures us that *Tropic of Cancer* "cannot fail to be moral finally, because the ferocity is radically moral." If ferocity be not its principal claim to morality, it hath no other. Yet the ferocity, here, is the symptom of its blind and irresponsible moral anarchy. He says no to everything except the random impulse of the senses.

Yet this is an awesome barrage of plaudits. Must dissenters crawl away rebuked? I think not. If the boys like it, let them have it. But let's keep the paean down to a yell. They have made *Tropic of Cancer*, this one-time object of tourist treasure-hunts among the Paris bookstalls, into all but a sacred artifact. If these gentlemen had united on the simple, unpretentious assertion that it is a good book, it would be easier to hold a discussion. But since they have gone so far in one direction, I will go so far in the other as to say it is not a good book. It is a sociologically and psychologically interesting outpouring of a one-time professional *enfant terrible*, by no means unselfconscious.

It is indeed significant, but I suspect I would not agree with Sir Herbert Read as to what its significance is. Yet the book, in its American edition, is with us. I see no reason why people who feel a distaste or disgust for it should fly into a hysteria to match Mr. Shapiro's. The whole thing is part of the larger phenomenon of the seriously—indeed tragically—undermined morale of the West, which I have analyzed elsewhere as resulting in part from a widespread loss of the Judeo-Christian image of man. Its American publishers, who most certainly calculated, "If we make it with *Lady Chatterley*, we'll try it with *Tropic of Cancer*," have brought off the gambit. Henry Miller is at least alive to reap some of the rewards, which the most ungenerous should not begrudge an author. So much for that.

Even with the publicity that always accompanies censorship struggles, *Lady Chatterley* at $6.00 and

Tropic of Cancer at $7.50, in the all too few real bookstores that our country boasts, are relatively harmless. The rub comes when they enter the cheap paperback mass market in drugstores and on newsstands. The champions of unrestricted publication (actually champions of unrestricted sales—which is not the same thing) are much given to saying it has never been proved that anyone was ever corrupted by a book. Yet no one can say that it is good to expose young people to the fringes of sexual experience while they are still groping toward the center; to saturate them with reading about the corrupt, the perverse, and the abnormal when they are not yet grounded in their developing adjustments to the natural and the normal.

Both *Chatterley* and *Tropic of Cancer* abound in images that are not desirable or constructive for the young mind. The power of images is greater than that of arguments in this area of concern. In Shaw's *Captain Brassbound's Conversion*, when the penny dreadfuls of Drinkwater, the cockney, are about to be cast into the fire, he pleads, "It's maw lawbrary, gavner. Downt burn 'em. . . . They formed maw mawnd. . . ." *Chatterley* and *Tropic of Cancer* are not helpful elements in forming the adolescent mind.

There is much expert scientific testimony about how relatively harmless are small doses of nuclear fallout. But no one argues that any of it is a positive good. I will not try to prove what psychological harm may be done to numbers of young (or other) readers by the massive cumulative and residual fall-out from *Lady Chatterley*, *Tropic of Cancer* and the increasing volume of the post-Chatterley deluge. But one thing is certain, it is no positive benefit to anybody and there is a massive, fetid pollution of the atmosphere. In England, Penguin Books, after their legal victory with *Lady Chatterley*, shed a tear publicly over the admittedly unfortunate aspect of much of its mass sale to adolescents—but they kept the presses rolling. As of the fall of 1961, 3,500,000 copies of the English edition had been sold. A Penguin spokesman estimated that without the trial publicity, they would have sold about 250,000. Again, the ironies of censorship. But there would not have been sales in the millions, and quite probably not 250,000, in an expensive hard-cover edition, had it been restricted to that.

Some American critics seemed to display as much breathless excitement over the new enlargement of freedom as some writers, and showed an equal precipitateness of response. We found Harvey Swados proclaiming in a review, immediately popped into a publisher's plug: "The liberation of our novelists to write freely of sexual matters is finally paying off. . . ." This has an excitingly promising sound, but alas, what did the pay-off prove to be? *Confessions of a Spent Youth*, by Vance Bourjaily. In it, a character somewhat coyly called U. S. D. Quincy led us on the familiar rounds of brothels, marijuana

parties, and miscellaneous sexual capers on several
continents in war and peace. That this well-worn
record, a retrogression for Mr. Bourjaily, should be
so received by Mr. Swados would suggest what I
know to be untrue, that it was the first American
novel he had seen after at least twenty years' retreat
in a desert.

In England, in the fall of 1961, a year after the
release of Lady Chatterley from durance, there was
no sign among the new novels of any post-Chatterley deluge comparable to that in the United States,
at least among books of serious literary claims. The
saddest fare in British bookstores is the abundance
of American trash published there, though even
some of that is editorially modified at no sacrifice
to integrity in work that had none to begin with.
Whatever post-Chatterley wave is there so far
reaches there from our own coasts.

Apparently the younger British writers, even the
angry ones, have a greater sense of mature restraint.
It may simply be that they are free of the obsession
with the sex-violence syndrome that haunts so much
of our writing. It may be that British publishers, too,
still preserve more of that good taste which Norman
Cousins so oddly attributed to the American publishers of *Tropic of Cancer*. It is true that some
British editors and publishers still are not afraid to
counsel a restraint which many American publishers

and editors refrain from doing either from a mistaken conception of their role or from simple cynicism.

The English showed a broader awareness than we
that there are complex implications in the Chatterley
case. The London *Times* remarked quietly, ". . . it
is difficult to see where the law will now be able to
make a stand." In terms that had no counterpart in
America, Gerald Gardiner, the counsel for Penguin
Books, himself stated:

> There is one thing about which I want to be quite
> plain, because in my submissions it is of some im-
> portance not only that you (the Jury) should real-
> ize this but that everybody should realize it. It is
> this: that no one should think that if the use of
> these words for this special purpose, by this par-
> ticular author, in this particular book, is legitimate,
> it will follow that these words can be used by any
> scribbler writing any kind of novel.

The House of Lords held a debate on a restrictive
motion arising out of the case; it was sometimes
comic in a Gilbertian way, but some things said were
cogent and valuable, notably the contribution of
Viscount Hailsham, who, in speaking earnestly of
how to cope with writers that one might dislike, dis-
approve of, or disagree with, noted:

> We cannot do so by prohibiting their works by an
> act of law. We have to . . . fight, and the battle
> must involve a willingness on our part to meet
> our enemies in the open; to defeat them in argu-

ment armed with the like weapons of tongue and pen which they themselves have selected, prepared to show that our own beliefs are more realistic and more rational than theirs. We shall not succeed in this day and age by prohibiting their works merely because we regard their opinions as detestable.

English literary journals, since the trial, have held broad symposia on the subject of literature and censorship, and a thoughtful Rede Lecture at Cambridge on the subject by Lord Radcliffe was brought out as a pamphlet by the University Press. England is more sensitively aware of and responsive to this problem and its complexity than are we—so far.

My concern about the post-Chatterley deluge is twofold. It is moral, since a moral anarchy—a "so what" or "anything goes"—is displayed in our literature, on a mass scale, which simply cannot be dismissed as without present and future deleterious effects. This moral appeal reaches relatively few in the professional literary field, though it does reach some. Secondly, my concern is artistic—and this should reach everyone. This wave is virulently bad for writing—and for reading. The insistent, burdensomely detailed sexual descriptions, the compulsive attempt to top previous high watermarks in sex or violence, make the reading of much fiction unbearably tedious for anyone who has not an insatiable psychic hunger for such vicarious and voyeuristic participation. It is becoming increasingly compulsive writing for compulsive reading. The searcher for such kicks used to skip through books looking for the hot parts. The other readers now must skip to find the passages between the repetitive, ritualistic set-pieces about sex. They are all the same. The individuality of the writer disappears in these bottomless bogs, just as, thirty years ago, the genuine individuality of Henry Miller was all but swamped by the mechanical repetition of shock words, while the simple mistook his use of them for individuality itself.

Who knows how long it will be before writers perceive this peril? That our best newer ones do is hearteningly evident. That not enough do is still painfully apparent. The balance between literary freedom and responsibility, with security from external censorship, can be achieved only by the combined wisdom and discretion of writers, editors, publishers, and critics. We are woefully slow in coming to solid grips with the problem in these, our own ranks. So long as we delay, our continued intransigence, our complacency that we are winning the big cases in court, our pointless goading to exasperation of the large body of non-literary opinion invite against us the actions of police, public officials, and puritanical moralists.

It is yet another irony that we fight censorship for fringe books while a major, serious, long-standing censorship problem is before us that we will not overcome soon. This is the censorship and bowdlerization in our public high schools of standard works, old and new, under attack from aggressive and incompetent pressure groups of a variety of kinds. This is a battle which is not to win freedom for a few individuals to sell for great profit a few notorious books. This struggle involves our freedom and breadth of education and the prospects for our general national literacy. I would like to see the zeal of writers and critics and the whole book trade brought to bear on this front.

The writer needs to mature his concept of his art, thinking less of what he is licensed to do than of what is worth doing. He should stop equating whatever emotion or sensation comes into his head with "truth" and consider that the mystery of truth is not reached glibly, off-the-cuff. It is a large, complex fabric. No one can say all that truth is, but it is possible to show what falls far short of it. To extol the truth of the obscene and scatalogical babblings that are a large part of *Tropic of Cancer* is childish. The scrawls daubed on the walls of a jakes are a reality, but not a truth; the distinction is one which needs to be made.

The role of the editor can be a fruitful one for both the writer and the publisher. He is not to dominate the writer, but to seek means to help the writer grow in self-realization and expression. To accept simply anything from the writer, on grounds of not interfering with his creative freedom, is to abdicate the editorial chair. A great deal of what is now published suggests that this abdication is widespread;

that in some offices little mature and balanced guidance or nurture, in taste or technique, is being brought to the development of talents. I am not suggesting that editors should muzzle any writers. I am saying that theirs is a front-line responsibility to help prevent the ultimate freedoms of the writer from becoming the current fad and fancy of any and all— an easy indulgence and path to notoriety if nothing else. That form of abdication that takes the plea, "But who is to judge?" is contemptible. People are judging—and must judge one way or another—at every stage of the literary operation. One might as well say, "Who is to judge whether to publish a book or not?" and publish every manuscript offered, passing the judgment along to somebody else.

As to the publisher—so concerned with freedom— let him remember his priceless freedom not to publish. He has obligations to resist publishing something simply because it will make money—though God knows that is asking him to stand at a level above the general merchandising ethics of the advertising era. He has at least the obligation to distinguish between a high-priced hard-cover edition and a mass-market paper edition of such works as *Lady Chatterley* and *Tropic of Cancer*. The assumption that if something can be published at the first level it must, or can, be published at the second does not follow. Publishers are the first to assert this about books that would not be profitable at the mass level. It may be that they will have to accept restraint about books that are not profitable to the public interest at the mass level. I hasten to emphasize that a *cause célèbre* such as *Lady Chatterley* is a drop in the bucket of this problem. Self-examination on this point by all publishers of hard- or paper-covered books is urgently needed. A self-regulation of the publishing trade, if it does not occur spontaneously (which would be best), may have to come about formally. It will be the best bulwark of everyone's freedom.

Editors and publishers function in group and organizational processes. Critics and reviewers (sometimes, but not always, the same), like other writers, function as individuals. There are many among them who operate solely in descriptive or explanatory terms. They will "explicate" a text and avoid involvement with the contents or implications of it. They use most carelessly the potent words "truth" and "compassion." There should always be an open engagement with the implications of a work as well as with its form and execution. I am not trying to restrict the premises of such judgment, but I am asking for such judgment on premises clearly and candidly developed. Also, I am asking for restraint. The absurd overpraise from creditable people lent to the promotion of *Lady Chatterley's Lover* and *Tropic of Cancer* makes a complete case for the need of a better sense of perspective in dealing with works that have become the center of publicity and moral controversy.

We who write, edit, publish and criticize (and some of us do, or have done, all four) must make ourselves the responsible referees of our literary freedom.

Thornton Wilder: the notation of the heart

Thornton Wilder has to his credit one of the greatest novels (*The Bridge of San Luis Rey*) and one of the greatest plays (*Our Town*) in this century's American writing. The rest of his body of work is consistent in quality. Success has visited him: he is a Pulitzer Prize winner in both fiction and drama; his plays have had packed houses; one of the novels was a best-seller. Yet, proportionate to his achievement, this man's stature is singularly overlooked or taken for granted in critical discussion. Until quite recently three of his five novels, all of them among the best American writing, had been out of print for years, and even *The Bridge* was not in hard covers.

He has had his due more among the drama critics than among those who study the art of prose fiction. In the books that talk of the contemporary American novel, where a fixed set of names is bandied about among a fixed set of critics, Wilder seldom is discussed. Malcolm Cowley is a notable exception, having written an excellent essay as Introduction to *A Thornton Wilder Trio* (1956), which brought back into print the first three novels.

This curious general neglect is partly because literary critics tend to inherit their subjects, passed along from one group to their successors. Within the contemporary field, one echelon seldom has the imagination to study someone whom the preceding echelon has ignored. Due to a socio-economic accident, Wilder was slighted by most critics practicing in the thirties and, accordingly, has not received attention since that time to any extent commensurate with his importance as a novelist.

The strange public history of *The Bridge of San Luis Rey*, its abrupt drop from acclaim to neglect, is worth pausing to examine. The book became a best-seller and a Pulitzer Prize winner. Malcolm Cowley remarks, wrongly I believe, that this success is "still a little hard to understand, for the best qualities of *The Bridge* are not those usually regarded as being popular." It "exactly fitted the mood of the moment, and nobody knows exactly why."

Public response often is surprising and hard to explain. The stylistic excellences and subtleties of thought and observation in this novel are not mass commodities. Yet greatness, which this book possesses, is never in itself a bar to popularity, given other viable elements. Shakespeare was a mass artist, and a substantial number of fine books make the best-seller list.

The Bridge is short and wonderfully lucid reading, with a simplicity of narrative hardly suggesting its extensive substrata. The question that the fall of the bridge thrust upon humble Brother Juniper: "Either we live by accident and die by accident, or we live by plan and die by plan"—in short, whether the events of life are chance or design—presents itself intensely, even agonizingly, at some time in almost every life. Thus it is that the Marquesa de Monte-mayor sometimes would be "dizzy with despair, and . . . would long to be taken from a world that had no plan in it." Consciously or unconsciously, from the French existentialists to the beat generation, this is a major psychic problem of the hydrogen age. The unlettered and the educated alike ponder the question in their own terms. It is a problem that presents itself as much amidst plenty as at any other time, which is why the book spoke to the anxieties beneath the boom of the flush twenties.

Another basis of the book's appeal is that its characters are sufficiently strange, colorful and remote to be fascinating, yet they are so universally human in their qualities that we can identify ourselves with them. Its original success and its re-emergence are gratifying, but not mysterious.

The book's abrupt eclipse (which engulfed all of Wilder's early novels) is a peculiar story. When the depression struck, the dreary wave of "social" novels, "protest" novels, "proletarian" or Marxist novels was ushered in and caused a corresponding literary depression, both in creation and criticism. What was possibly the best single book of that genre, *The Grapes of Wrath*, does not survive the passing of its topicality as well as *The Bridge* survives its temporary, circumstantial eclipse. I am one of many who came of age in the early thirties, heard *The Bridge* spat upon as bourgeois, escapist, popular pap, and had to find it for myself after depression and war had passed and writers had again discovered that the problems of man are not narrowly topical, or uniquely and exclusively centered on the masses, on workers, or even on soldiers.

Wilder is unique among modern American novelists for possessing in the highest degree certain qualities currently undervalued and hence desperately needed among us. No one of his countrymen rests his work upon such an understructure of broad scholarship, cultivation and passion for the beauty and integrity of the English language. This equipment, rare in our time, gives tone to his work, especially the novels, and yet brings with it no taint of pedantry. To find work equally rich in allusion and grounded in humane learning, we must turn to English-born Aldous Huxley, although Wilder employs these attributes even more gracefully and unobtrusively than he. In a period when literary honors are bestowed often upon the craftless, the semiliterate and uncultivated, and in which the Yahoo has become hero, we need to recall that we have Wilder working among us. He helps to redeem the time.

He is notable for his versatility. Although he is not the only man writing both the novel and the play, no one else has written both at such a level of excellence, in such a marked diversity of modes, or in such form-renewing and form-extending ways as mark his work in the two media.

Wilder is a conspicuous exception to the common generalization that American writers tend to be youthful, writing of and from youth and immaturity, failing to mature in art as they age in years. He juxtaposes his always mature vision of life and character to our predominantly adolescent literature, while his range is greater than that of those established men who are most nearly his peers. There is an immense spread between the sophistication of *The Cabala* and the homely simplicity of *Our Town,* and Wilder is comfortably at home in both.

He is neither compulsive in his choice of material and method nor conditioned by some warped piping from a private clinical world. His view of life and behavior is broadly encompassing and humanely compassionate in the only true compassion, which is blended of sympathetic perception and clearly defined values.

He has the highest development and conscious control of style—having no close rival among Americans in this respect—yet he spelled out the limits of style in *The Bridge,* in a passage about the Conde's relish for the famous letters of the Marquesa de Montemayor (which are like those of Mme. de Sévigné):

> . . . he thought that when he had enjoyed the style he had extracted all their richness and intention, missing (as most readers do) the whole purport of literature, which is the notation of the heart. Style is but the faintly contemptible vessel in which the bitter liquid is recommended to the world. The Marquesa would even have been astonished to learn that her letters were very good, for such authors live always in the noble weather of their own minds and those productions which seem remarkable to us are little better than a day's routine to them.

It is in this "whole purport of literature . . . the notation of the heart" that Wilder's genius is felt, and the flexible grace and individuality that attend his work in both his chosen media proceed from that "noble weather" of his own mind.

The novels are dazzlingly epigrammatic—a word that often carries with it a suggestion of glibness that does not fit this work. The epigram is a stylistic device, a perfectly shaped single thought, calculated to arrest attention and then, at its best, to start thought moving in a fresh direction. Such ability to shape and state things is sometimes given to shallow minds who waste it on minor witticism. In Wilder this gift is coupled with penetrating perception and wisdom. It helps him to communicate the depth and sharpness in which he sees character, motivation and impulse, and the significance that he discerns in things.

Wilder's work is permeated by a profound mystical and religious sensibility—too mature to war upon or sneer at orthodoxy, too creative to fit snugly in its confines. His vision and celebration of man are harmonious with Christian humanism. He gives us a *creature*, touched with the divine image, but scarred and maimed somewhat in his human state, perishable in his flesh and eternal in his soul; a creature variously perverse and responsible, despicable and indomitable, vulgar and rarefied. The separateness of these attributes remains blurred in Wilder's work as it is blurred in the creature and in the creature's self-understanding. Applying here some words from the Foreword to his first volume of short plays, *The Angel That Troubled the Waters*, "there has seldom been an age in literature when such a vein was less welcome and less understood."

He has been publishing and producing intermittently since 1926, and there is no reason to suppose that we have heard the last from him. His productive years, to date, span the time from his twenties to his late fifties, so he has been walking in step with his century. The reference of his work is always universal, regardless of its period identification. In times of depression and war he has not occupied himself with the obviously topical that commands attention sometimes to the temporary exclusion of all else. His nearest approach to the topical—the perennial topicality of the catastrophic—was in *The Skin of Our Teeth*, cast in such imaginative terms as to baffle literal minds.

Wilder is absorbed, always, with one or more of what, in *The Ides of March*, Caesar calls "the first questions which one puts to life itself." Or, as in *The Woman of Andros*, "How does one live? . . . What does one do first?" His answer is: one loves, if one can.

Of the master ideas or themes, threaded through and through the whole body of Wilder's work, certainly that of love is foremost. He is concerned with identifying its nature and its kinds, the modes of its operation, and the follies and waste associated with it. His is a conspicuous depth of insight at a time when many novelists have lost, or repudiated, the knowledge of love, offering violences, abuses and perversions of the body as substitutes for love rather than as violations or corruptions of it. In such modes, even the nature and meaning of simple passion itself are distorted, and the limited range of passion is unremarked.

In one of the most luminous passages of *The Bridge*, Wilder looks into the heart of the Perichole, who is marred by smallpox and convinced that love is forever lost to her.

This assumption that she need look for no more devotion now that her beauty had passed proceeded from the fact that she had never realized any love save love as passion. Such love, though it expends itself in generosity and thoughtfulness, though it give birth to visions and to great poetry, remains among the sharpest expressions of self-interest. Not until it has passed through a long servitude, through its own self-hatred, through mockery, through great doubts, can it take its place among the loyalties. Many who have spent a lifetime in it can tell us less of love than the child that lost a dog yesterday.

One of his three-minute plays, exercises in that compression that Wilder prizes so highly and has mastered so well, the play that lends its title to a whole volume, *The Angel That Troubled the Waters* (1928), contains the words: "In Love's service only the wounded soldiers can serve."

In the polished and precocious first novel, *The Cabala* (1926), two of his characters, Astrée-Luce and the Cardinal, reach a terrible spiritual impasse. When they

   . . . discovered that they were living in a world where such things could be forgiven, that no actions were too complicated but that love could understand, or dismiss them, on that day they began their lives all over again.

The failure to love is the failure to realize life. Wilder is pained at how we fumble love, fail in realization, often through no worse a sin than perennial human blindness—that proverbial blindness that is never so great as in those who will not see.

So in that poignant scene of *Our Town* in which

the dead Emily ventures to return to live over again her twelfth birthday (a scene anticipated in *The Woman of Andros*), there comes the girl's anguished cry, "Let's look at one another." And a moment later, ". . . it goes so fast. We don't have time to look at one another . . . I didn't realize. So all that was going on and we never noticed." Then follows the great question and answer:

> EMILY: Do any human beings ever realize life while they live it?—every, every minute?
>
> STAGE MANAGER: No. (*Pause*) The saints and poets, maybe—they do some.

It is the waste of love and life that pains Chrysis, the woman of Andros: "She did not realize that this wasting of love in fretfulness was one of the principal activities on the planet."

The crowning of this theme of love is in *The Bridge*. For the gentle Juniper there is no reward but burning for his naïve attempt to fathom the secrets of God and "surprise His intentions in a pure state." Unresolved though it must necessarily remain, this question of chance or design gives shape to the novel, from the opening chapter, "Perhaps an Accident," to the closing one, "Perhaps an Intention." Yet if Juniper's search for an intention fails, Wilder still develops subtly for us the possibility of an intention of some kind on the part of One Who moves in a mysterious way, in a design infinitely more intricate than the too simple equation the monk had sought (like Job) between a man's moral qualities and the things that happen to him. There was a cryptic, unexplained saying of Jesus to his disciples: "Think you that those eighteen upon whom the tower in Siloam fell were the greatest sinners in Jerusalem?"

Whether it is the reason for the event or not, there is indeed a sense in which, as Juniper had speculated, each of the five lives lost made up a perfect whole when the bridge fell. The Marquesa, Pepita, Esteban, Uncle Pio and even, in a special sense, the boy Jaime, who must venture out to face the world with the burden of epilepsy—each had been through a crisis of decision and commitment, or moral self-realization and responsibility, and above all, a crisis of love. Accordingly, perhaps, now each can be permitted release—for death is often so viewed by Wilder, without negating his affirmation of life.

Consider where the five lives stand as the disaster happens. The Marquesa has experienced a transformation through self-discovery. The girl, Pepita, through her simple devotion to the Abbess, has opened the Marquesa's eyes to her own selfishness and self-pity. She knows, now, that her empty religious observances, her drunkenness, her nagging demands upon her daughter, all are the products of her own pride and vanity. She empties her heart, in a great letter to her daughter, and whispers, "Let me live now . . . Let me begin again." It is the will that counts—after this, the bridge. . . .

The youthful Pepita has suffered from her separation from the adored Abbess. To her she writes the letter so influential in its effect upon the Marquesa. The tone is like the great prayer, "Not my will, but Thine, be done." Even so, Pepita tears up the letter, with its request for a return to the convent, saying, "It wasn't . . . it wasn't . . . brave." She has made her wish submit to her duty, and after this, the bridge. . . .

Esteban has mastered the grief for his brother; the grief so great that he assumed, for a while, the name of his brother. If he was Manuel, Manuel could not be dead. Under the kind help of Captain Alvarado, and after the attempt at suicide, Esteban at last makes the painful struggle back to the acceptance of reality, the acceptance of life without his brother, the acceptance of the mysterious will of God. And after this, the bridge. . . .

Uncle Pio, that tenderly worldly man, touched both with the world's cynicism and the love of art and all things beautiful, has made his final act of loyalty toward the Perichole. With a kindly "cruelty" he forces her, in her withdrawal from people, to listen to him and to permit him to "borrow" her child, in order to educate him properly. This was an act of disinterested love of a kind the Perichole could scarcely believe. And after this, the bridge. . . .

Perhaps to the Perichole's son, Jaime, the event is a merciful release. The child, who is very young, and who suffers both pain and shame from his epilepsy, bravely ventures from the shelter of his retreat with his mother, into the world for which Uncle Pio will try to prepare him. Even as they approach the bridge, he wrestles with the shame of feeling that the convulsions are about to come upon him, here in a public place. And then, the bridge. . . .

Thus the possibility of death as a gift to these five at the end of decision cannot be overlooked.

If any intention underlies the fall of the bridge, it cannot involve only the lives ended—it must involve also the lives remaining. So it is that Captain Alvarado, the Perichole, the daughter of the Marquesa, and Mother Maria del Pilar, all are enlarged in grace and comprehension. It is of the love of God toward man that the Abbess speaks, saying to herself, "Now learn, learn at last that anywhere you may expect grace."

The true burden of the book is disclosed in its final line:

> There is a land of the living and a land of the dead and the bridge is love, the only survival, the only meaning.

This is the bridge that does not fall.

Human life as Wilder shows it is a web of folly, faith and tenacity. The folly is always present—a constant in the human character. As Dolly Levi says, in *The Matchmaker*,

. . . there comes a moment in everybody's life
when he must decide whether he'll live among
human beings or not—a fool among fools or a fool
alone.

In *Our Town* the Stage Manager reflects:

Wherever you come near the human race, there's
layers and layers of nonsense. . . .

Folly, both of the lighter and the grimmer orders, is
threaded through that fantastic synopsis of the race's
history, *The Skin of Our Teeth*, summed up in
Sabina's cry,

We're all just as wicked as we can be, and that's
the God's truth.

But Wilder is a gentle, not a savage, observer of
folly. He blends folly with faith in the extravagant,
picaresque, evangelical adventures of George Brush,
the hero of *Heaven's My Destination* (1935). This
fourth novel is startlingly different, in manner,
method and material, from the other novels. Its tone
is that of his plays, and I have wondered if, at some
stage in its gestation, it may have hovered between
the two forms. It is high parody, in somewhat the
vein, and with the same deceptive simplicity, as *Can-
dide* or *Joseph Andrews*. To descend somewhat in
levels of comparison, there is even a touch of the
Sinclair Lewis of *The Man Who Knew Coolidge*.

George, who is a textbook salesman and evangelist
extraordinary, is the innocent fool, or the foolish in-

nocent, in the kindliest sense of both the noun and the adjective. He is striving to be the fool in Christ, sowing the inevitable amazement, consternation and wrath that must ensue when Christ's fool runs at large among the worldly wise. This, in dark tones, was the concept underlying Dostoyevsky's *The Idiot.*

Wilder's George is also "the perfectly logical man," fulfilling conviction in action, practicing his preaching. To understand him it is necessary to observe the quotation from *The Woman of Andros* that Wilder uses as a text in the front matter of *Heaven's My Destination:* "Of all the forms of genius, goodness has the longest awkward age."

For all the sophistication that underlies the creation of George Brush—indeed that was essential to it —Wilder loves this innocent and will not consent that we should do otherwise. His is the awkward age of a true goodness. Simple, it is; stupid, it is not. Nor is it easy. George suffers his own bitter crises of faith, and his occasional cry of "I don't want to live" is a genuine anguish. Among the most subtle and interesting devices of the book is the unseen figure called Father Pasziewski, seemingly comic in his context, but who becomes, through the simple bequest of a silver spoon, the instrument to free George from his darkest night of the soul. In this border terrain of folly and faith, Wilder sounds a cautionary note to the George Brushes of the world through Judge Carberry:

Go slow; go slow. . . . The human race is pretty
stupid . . . Doesn't do any good to insult'm. Go
gradual.

Reflecting the perennial tension between faith and
reason, we are told that Astrée-Luce, in *The Cabala*,
has "goodness without intelligence." Her frustration
is that "Sainthood is impossible without obstacles and
she never could find any." Yet this wholly nonintel-
lectual woman is capable of "remarkable penetrating
judgments, judgments that proceeded from the in-
tuition without passing through the confused corridors of our reason."

The Cardinal Vaini, in the same book, who makes
a grave miscalculation as a spiritual director in dealing with her, has his own soul crisis after being retired to Italy from his lifetime work in China.

Living is fighting and away from the field the most
frightening changes were taking place in his mind.
Faith is fighting, and now that he was no longer
fighting he couldn't find his faith anywhere.

It is this same Cardinal, by the way, in Wilder's early
anticipation of the modern dilemma of blurred values
in the midst of an advanced technology, who says,
with wry reservations about the attainments of the
age:

You want me to compliment you because you have
broken the atom and bent light? Well, I do, I do.

But whether the follies of man be those of the
subtle mind or the simple, or even those of the

wicked, there is an amazing tenacity in the creature. It is this tenacity that is celebrated in *The Skin of Our Teeth* (1942), one of the most wildly creative, antic and imaginative plays of the modern theatre. It stunned to befuddlement its early audiences, but it has captured increasing command over playgoers ever since, here and abroad, as the appalling march of modern society has made us more and more sensitive to the threatening chaos. Wilder has observed, correctly, that it plays best in times of crisis. He says, by the way, that it is heavily indebted to *Finnegans Wake*, which is apparent, and is perhaps sufficient rebuke to me for an abiding prejudice against that work.

The play pours out for us, in tumbling fantasy, the total, sprawling, blundering chronicle of Man. We see it in a multiple vision which superimposes the Pleistocene, the Flood and the ages since, upon present-day New Jersey.

Mr. and Mrs. Antrobus (the pun on *anthropos*—Mr. and Mrs. Man—is inescapable), the complaining but durable Sabina, and the children, including the troublesome Cain (renamed Henry, since his trouble over Abel, but still the same boy), are indomitable. Mrs. Antrobus, at the end, amidst the wreckage of war, cries to her husband:

> . . . the only thought we clung to was that you were going to bring something good out of this suffering. In the night, in the dark, we'd whisper about it, starving and sick.—Oh George, you'll have

to get it back again. Think! What else kept us
alive all these years? Even now, it's not comfort
we want. We can suffer whatever's necessary; only
give us back that promise.

George Antrobus says:

All I ask is the chance to build new worlds and
God has always given us that. And has given us
voices to guide us, and the memory of our mistakes to warn us.

He turns the leaves of a book.

We've come a long ways. We've learned. We're
learning. And the steps of our journey are marked
for us here.

As in this play, so in all his work Wilder delights
in making free with time and space, as well as all sequences and juxtapositions of history. He treats time
not so much in the Greek way, as cyclic, but as if all
time is always still present. We might call it the si-
multaneity of all time—a concept which will be seen
in the novels of Charles Williams. *Our Town* moves
about freely in the time stream. In one early remark
of the Stage Manager, present, future, past, and historical present are combined in a single sentence.

First automobile's going to come along in about
five years—belonged to Banker Cartwright, our
richest citizen . . . lives in the big white house up
on the hill.

Wilder also chooses models for characters across a
broad range of time, reshuffling them blandly from

one age to another. He translates the Marquise de Sévigné from seventeenth-century France to eighteenth-century Peru, to reincarnate her as the Marquesa de Montemayor. He gives us the dying John Keats in twentieth-century Rome, and embodies there, in *The Cabala*, certain of the Olympian gods in latter-day decline, and calls up the shade of Virgil. In *The Ides of March*, we find the extraordinary, bedridden American playwright, Edward Sheldon, on the isle of Capri, metamorphosed into the fearfully maimed Lucius Mamilius Turrinus. This most intimate friend and confidant of Caesar, once well favored of the gods but now brought low, is, like Sheldon, mentor and dispenser of wisdom to a host of talents more fortunate than himself.

Applying this free movement as a playwright, Wilder has helped to liberate the stage of our period from the strait jacket of the box set. He discusses this aspect of his intentions in the Preface to *Three Plays* (1957), which is a valuable, brief essay on the relationship of things to themes in the theatre. The essence of his dramaturgy he expresses in words from Molière as "a platform and a passion or two."

This is true presentational theatre. It *presents* something to us, quite frankly as make-believe, demanding full participation from us in achieving its effects, which become all the stronger because we make ourselves a part of them. This important relationship between the people on the stage and the audience makes *Our Town* more effective on a stage than it was as a movie with realistic scenes, and with the Stage Manager reduced to a mere commentator.

What could be a more frank expression of pure theatre than the act of the Stage Manager (himself borrowed from the Chinese drama) pushing out trellises, and saying,

> There's some scenery for those who think they have to have scenery.

This same engaging candor is displayed in the Stage Manager's dismissal of the actors in certain sequences as soon as they have shown us all that is needed. We understand that this scene could go on indefinitely, but that we've had enough for immediate purposes. So he interrupts, saying,

> That'll do. That'll do. Thank you very much. . . .

Altogether these techniques, far from weakening the absorbing qualities of the play, lend it an added dimension, a special fascination, like a glass-cased clock in which you can see the works.

Certain of his one-act plays are preparatory studies for the major dramatic works. They test the essential "round" pattern that characterizes *Our Town* and *The Skin of Our Teeth*, the spirit of which might be vulgarized as "here we go again." Thus the short plays are a valuable study in the development of technique and idea, as a set of variations in music may be seen sometimes as part of the growth of a work.

The Long Christmas Dinner, which Paul Hindemith has made into an opera, telescopes ninety years and several generations of a family into a single meal, as *The Skin of Our Teeth* traverses all the ages of man in three acts. The latter play's procession of planets and hours has a trial run in *Pullman Car Hiawatha.* And in this, and in *The Happy Journey to Trenton and Camden,* plain chairs are made to serve as whatever setting is needed. *Pullman Car Hiawatha* also has a versatile, chatty Stage Manager, all in anticipation of *Our Town.* The pullman car stops at "Grover's Corners," but the long later play relocates this from Ohio to New Hampshire. The emotional final sequence of *The Happy Journey* resembles in tone the intimate home scenes of *Our Town.* Finally, in *Pullman Car,* a dead young woman makes an itemized good-bye speech to persons and places anticipating Emily's tender good-bye to the world and Grover's Corners.

In speaking of these experiments in time and space, Wilder defined the purpose that informs all of his work in all media—the attempt "to capture not verisimilitude but reality." This is pregnant with counsel for an overliteral age of letters, bogged down often in the narrowest naturalism, or worse still and even more prevalent, pseudo naturalism. Wilder's is that truer realism, unconfined in its means, seeking, as he said of *Our Town,* to "find a value above all price for the smallest events in our daily life." He achieved this aim uniquely in that play. In one of the Stage Manager's long discourses, the "cornerstone" speech in Act One, he sums up one of the universal qualities literature attempts to capture: the sense, in any era, that ". . . this is the way we were in our growing up and in our marrying and in our doctoring and in our living and in our dying."

Wilder has a deep affinity for the ancient world; and apart from much allusion to it in all the works, he has turned to it for time and place in two of his novels. He did this first in the gentle, lyric, lovely *Woman of Andros*, set on the isles of Greece in that time when "the land that was soon to be called Holy prepared in the dark its wonderful burden."

It is in *The Ides of March* (1948) that we get his most ambitious image of the ancient world, in the most intricately constructed and ambitious of all the novels. Its spaciousness of concept creates a sense of a much larger work, physically, than it is in fact. Nowhere is his self-avowed "passion for compression" more successfully operable.

Here he takes his familiar liberties with time sequence and literal, factual matters, but he gives us a sense of a living Rome and a living Caesar. Through the difficult and adroitly practiced device of imaginary letters and documents, he evokes the most complex Caesar that I know in any work of art. This Julius's closest relative is Shaw's—that is, both are created in indifference to historical actuality as idealizations of a point of view (a device of the classical historians as well, as witness Herodotus's famous dia-

logue between Solon and Croesus). These Caesars
have in common a detached, deliberative calm, and
the relationship of each of them to Cleopatra is dominated primarily by a "passion for teaching." Yet
Shaw's Caesar is a one-dimensional cartoon, withal
brilliant, while Wilder's is complexly human with
the special dimensions of genius.

Caesar's reflections on Roman society cut sharply
into our own.

> . . . the ostentation of vulgarity has become a po-
> litical factor with which I must deal. The plebeian
> world is ameliorable in itself, but what can I do
> with a plebeian aristocracy? . . . it's now smart to
> talk pure *pleb*.

The book is rich in its meditations upon liberty
and rule, freedom and responsibility, interest and dis-
interest in public actions. The dual study of Caesar
and Catullus (wholly as fanciful as Solon and Croesus) puts before us the statesman vis-à-vis the poet.
Catullus is, in a sense, one face of this Caesar, who
says,

> . . . one of the things in this world that I most
> envy is the endowment from which springs great
> poetry. To the great poets I ascribe the power to
> gaze fixedly at the whole of life and bring into
> harmony that which is within and that which is
> without them.

Is not this the transcendent aim of the great statesman?

I think there is only one solitude greater than that of the military commander and of the head of state and that is the poet's—for who can advise him in that unbroken succession of choices which is a poem? It is in this sense that responsibility is liberty; the more decisions that you are forced to make alone, the more you are aware of your freedom to choose. I hold that we cannot be said to be aware of our minds save under responsibility. . . .

The Ides of March is a text so rich that it requires exploration rather than reading.

Wilder's love of the ancient world, however, is not a flight from the modern one. He has been wise about that from the first. The returning American narrator of *The Cabala* is advised by Virgil, as he leaves Rome: "The secret is to make a city, not to rest in it."

Perhaps, finally, with Wilder, after love comes beauty as the second great theme. He said, in the Foreword to *The Angel That Troubled the Waters*, speaking of religion as a subject in art, ". . . in these matters beyond logic, beauty is the only persuasion." He has made it the instrument of his own persuasion in all matters. This may be what has shaped his style. The stamp of taste and the sure sense of the precise and subtle gradations of meaning that come with mastery of language and that are the essence of beauty in the written word are firmly in his possession.

And with beauty comes praise. Praise of life is constant with him. He knows the sometime kindness of death. He has the vision of something beyond death. He can remark the pain of living, as he gives words to the shade of Virgil:

> Are you still alive? Alive? How can you endure it? All your thoughts are guesses, all your body is shaken with breath, all your senses are infirm and your mind ever full of the fumes of some passion or another. Oh, what misery to be a man. Hurry and die!

Yet, like a descant over all his melodies is the note of praise.

One of the dead, a woman, in the poignant dual vision of the famous graveyard scene in *Our Town*, is reminded of childbirth, and remarks, almost with a laugh,

> I'd forgotten all about that. My, wasn't life awful
>   (*With a sigh*)
> —and wonderful?

Simon Stimson, in the same scene, echoes Virgil's words above:

> That's what it was to be alive. To move about in a cloud of ignorance . . . to spend and waste time as though you had a million years . . . to be always at the mercy of one self-centered passion or another.

Mrs. Gibbs rebuffs him:

> Simon Stimson, that ain't the whole truth and you know it.

Emily herself, retreating from the pain of her return on her twelfth birthday, ends her cry of farewell to all people, places and things of life, with:

> Oh, earth, you're too wonderful for anybody to realize you.

In *The Cabala*, the narrator visits the bedside of the dying poet (Keats transposed). He wounds the suffering man unintentionally by a casual slur upon Chapman's Homer, and so

> discovered that he was hungry for hearing things praised . . . the poet wanted before he left the strange world to hear some portion of it praised.

Again, in *The Ides of March*, Caesar at the bedside of another dying poet, Catullus, observes:

> I am no stranger to deathbeds. To those in pain one talks about themselves, to those of clear mind one praises the world that they are quitting. There is no dignity in leaving a despicable world and the dying are often fearful life was not worth the efforts it had cost them. I am never short of subjects to praise.

Thornton Wilder, wise observer and celebrant of life, speaks in the dying courtesan, Chrysis, of Andros, as she is making "the most exhausting of all our adventures . . . that journey down the long corridors of the mind to the last halls where belief is enthroned." As she goes this course, she reflects:

> I have known the worst that the world can do to

me, and . . . nevertheless I praise the world and all living.

So, likewise, does Wilder, in the total body of this humane notation of the heart that is his work. In this shrewd, sometimes caustic observation of genus Homo and his history, we find one of the most searching, balanced and mature visions of ourselves as Man that any American writer offers us.

Gladys Schmitt: "Jacob and the angel"

Gladys Schmitt stands among our contemporary American writers with the solid achievement of seven novels, published between 1942 and 1961. None of them has failed to command respectful attention; most have received notable praise; three can be set among the outstanding books of her generation and seem certain to be read for a long while to come. It is surprising that no survey of this whole body of work has been made before now; it is overdue.

The development of her writing followed an interesting alternating pattern. It began with *The Gates of Aulis* (1942), a long, ambitious modern novel. It was hailed in superlatives, Stanley Hyman calling its writing "astonishingly good . . . unbelievable in a first novel," and Whit Burnett asserting, "She is the American Proust." In 1946 came a work of an utterly different kind, the biblical novel *David the King*. If it surprised the devotees of the first book, it found its own instant praise. Ludwig Lewisohn declared it "one of the most distinguished books written in America in my time," while Louis Untermeyer likened it to the Joseph tetralogy of Thomas Mann. Fast upon its heels, in 1947, came *Alexandra*, another modern story, a rather slight book but sufficient to induce Diana Trilling to compare its author to Willa Cather; 1952 brought *Confessors of the Name*, a vast story arising out of the persecution of Christians under the Roman Emperor Decius in the third century. Among its accolades, Gilbert Highet noted that "Few writers understand even their own time as well as Miss Schmitt understands that almost-Christian Rome." *The Persistent Image* (1955) and *A Small Fire* (1957), both modern, received with more muted praise, broke the precise pattern of alternation. In 1961, clearly long in the making, came her *Rembrandt*, in some ways the proudest and most perfected of her works to date.

Prior to *Rembrandt*, *David the King* and *Confessors of the Name* stood out as much the major works, although the lesser ones would be a credit to any writer. The predominance of these two may have delayed a systematic appraisal of her work. There is a tendency among our critics to overlook or deprecate what we are forced by prevailing usage to call "historical," "biblical" or "biographical" novels. Because much shoddy stuff or merely competent hack work is so labeled, it takes the reputation of a

Thomas Mann or a Sholem Asch to persuade some people of the literary respectability of the forms. Gladys Schmitt, working in all three categories with her illuminating way of seeing the past, demonstrates that we should not allow a hyphenation of the novel to obscure our view of what the gifted artist can achieve in any variety of this protean medium.

A certain silt of canonical critical opinion tends to drift around much-analyzed writers. In approaching fresh ones we are newly reminded that criticism is the journal of an individual's encounters with works of art. It is not an irresponsible, unrooted subjective reaction, for the history, range, forms and techniques of the medium are the basis for some demonstrable objective standards. Yet criticism *is* reaction, *is* opinion, *is* liking or disliking, however elaborate the equipment brought to it. As I attempt a brief survey of the whole of Gladys Schmitt's work I am conscious that at the center of my vision are the three big books that are not modern in setting. Although her demonstrated merits cannot be confined to these, although there are many threads of relationship among all her books, I shall probably never read one of her four modern novels again, but *David, Confessors* and *Rembrandt* I shall revisit often.

It is the excellence and magnitude of the people portrayed, the scope of the vision of man that illuminates them, that makes the difference in the excellence and magnitude of these three books compared to the other four. An analogy can be drawn from *A Small Fire*. Frieda Hartmann, its narrator, speaks of "the difference between my flat, dry speaking voice and the ardent outward flow of my singing voice." This expresses the difference I find between much of Miss Schmitt's writing in the modern books and the passionate soaring in the others.

A separate essay could be, and no doubt some day will be, written about the modern novels of Gladys Schmitt. My present purpose—an introductory essay to explore a few primary aspects of her total work and thought to date—imposes stringent limitations upon me. It projects the historical books into heightened prominence. It precludes the study of many values within individual novels of either category—details of her polished craftsmanship as well as subtleties of characterization and thought that would require close analysis of the separate books. Other studies, in the future, certainly will make up for this lack.

Her modern novels present people subjective to the point of sickliness. There are neuroses, indeed psychoses, to be noted in her historical books, from the madness of Saul to the jealous frustration of Rembrandt's sister Lysbeth. But the frame is more vast; the stature, the magnitude of the whole, makes an enormous difference in net effect and value. Moreover, the modern books set forth their stories subjectively in the first person, in two instances, and from the point of view of deeply subjective personalities in the other two.

The atmosphere in her contemporary scenes often is too close for my taste, stifling with its sensory and psychological minutiae. This is the aspect that caused her to be called a modern Proust. I admit frankly a lack of love for Proust and thus am disqualified from appreciating Proust in her. The historical books are essentially objective, by contrast, yet fully as sensitive in perception. Indeed, they achieve even greater penetrations, for an objective sensitivity sees farther than a subjective one, being less confined by a self or a series of selves.

Also, there is an insistent overt psychologizing in the modern books that obscures her enormous power to touch the universal. However soundly grounded the broad psychological assumptions may be, they tend to stunt character by implied clinical explanation of it. Sometimes the stature of the characters in the modern books seems insufficient to justify the minute care expended on their portraits. The people of her historical books live and grow more simply and directly, although they spring from the same mind enriched by all the knowledge that is insufficiently assimilated in the others.

The first novel, *The Gates of Aulis*, is a major effort, illuminated at times by her finest qualities. Compared to it, the other modern novels seem to be breathers. It is as if she has been on long expeditions into the hinterlands of the spirit toward the sources of the rivers of life, and that between-times she must relax into the more commonplace and immediate. Yet these books contain the elements of her great themes and preoccupations, quiescent, germinating, waiting for another powerful surge.

Not to set confines upon her range of interest, but as a structure for examination, I suggest three constant themes of her work. These are: love, in a diversity of modes; the creative process, studied in its sources and behavior in several arts (including living); and God, under Whose shadow, in her finest books, the other subjects are always seen. A sub-theme in relation to both God and love, is abnegation or sacrifice, seen both in healthy and sickly forms. The sick self-giving of Ellie Hasselman in *The Gates of Aulis* stands in contrast to the devotion of Hendrijke Stoffels in *Rembrandt* or to the broader giving of the Elder Moyses in *Confessors of the Name*.

In the historical works, but not the modern ones save in parts of *The Gates of Aulis*, she achieves the classical attribute of compelling magnitude. Also, qualities that characterize her treatment of all her preoccupying themes and the drawing of all her characters are a sense of nobility, an awareness of the ambivalence of almost all emotion, an authentic compassion and that smaller province of the same kingdom, tenderness.

The Gates of Aulis treats of love sickened and incapacitated by a neurotic compulsion toward sacrifice. Its two main figures, Ellie Hasselman and her brother Carl, out of a Lutheran heritage that is not an active agent in their immediate family environment, both suffer the conviction that love cannot be permitted, that the flesh cannot be fulfilled, unless tendered upon a kind of sacrificial stone. It is essentially a lack of conviction of their own worth and right.

The title derives from the bold attempt, more important than the sum of the achievement, to construct a vast metaphor from the motif of Iphigenia willingly offering herself as a sacrifice on the altars at Aulis, that the gods might be placated and the Greek fleet granted winds to sail for Troy. Ellie Hasselman is an Iphigenia with no Agamemnon, herself both willing and performing the sacrifice.

Ellie, after a long reflection upon several generations of her forebears (in itself the finest writing achievement in the book, anticipating Miss Schmitt's later powers), concludes: ". . . we are all alike in this: all of us sought and found a sacrificial stone." Her reverie elaborates the analogy:

> Wait—crown the dream with analysis, wash the vision in reason, expose the sea-weed of our sorrows to the clean sun so that it will be acceptable to sane and waking men. I cannot excuse our frailty by saying that we were destined for a stone. With logic I can say only that we sought a stone. God-possessed or devil-ridden, passionate or serene, fragile or mighty—in this flaw of the spirit we were and are the same. This is the inheritance that

passes to the third and fourth generations. Brother, as Iphigenia went to Aulis to die willingly upon a sacrificial altar so that a fleet might be saved and so that she herself might be reborn, so we will go to Aulis, you and I.

Unfortunately, Ellie has no fleet to launch. Her stone is the bed on which she comforted two feeble lovers, one quickly dead of tuberculosis, one a burnt-out industrialist and minor patron of the arts who re-establishes a waning potency with her and leaves her, to marry a more fleshly creature of his own set. The spell that always commands Ellie's love is the sight of a naked, unappetizing need in others; metaphorically, she is a kisser of lepers, upon impulses less well directed than those of Saint Francis. By all of this, her art as a painter is stifled or twisted.

Carl Hasselman is presumed to have capacities that at no time are wholly convincing. He represents an authentic type all too drearily projected. In the depths of the Great Depression this young sociologist falls under the hypnotic spell of the Luciferian Professor Maurer, who takes him up as a protégé. Maurer, theatrically overdrawn as a Communist who by the end has modulated into a Fascist (at a time when Communists were considered a little bit all right, but Fascists clearly bad), confirms Carl's feeling that it is decent to love humanity as abstract masses but somehow corrupting to become involved with persons. As Ellie observes, "For people in general, he'll carry hot coals to the edge of the earth;

but he wouldn't burn his hands for any man. . . ."
This is far from that excellent Christian concept that
Christ came not to save "men" but to save each man.
(Miss Schmitt shows her awareness of the fallacy of
abstract love in all her books, but perhaps nowhere
more pointedly than in a reflection on the teachings
of Plotinus, in *Confessors of the Name*.)

At the end of a long self-torture, Carl and Ellie,
both at a suicidal verge, break through to save each
other. Carl is wrenched out of his shell of abstract
concern and forced physically to drag the real Ellie
of bone and blood up from the gates of death when
she has flung herself into rock-filled waters. Gasping
in the recovered life, she cried, "If I'd thought you'd
come after me . . . you last of all . . . If I'd known
that there was still that much compassion left in this
world, I'd never have gone down. . . ."

This ambitious, overextended, but sometimes
powerful novel is a bit pat in its ending: Ellie, free
of the sacrificial compulsion, is painting at full power
again, and Carl is vigorously in love with a well-
fleshed girl who has long been waiting for him to
break out of the wraps. Yet the book has valid insights into disorders of love, although less than an
adequate concept about their remedy. Whatever its
faults, it was a striking debut.

David the King, from its first page, displays a controlled, eloquent and unfaltering prose. The central
portrait is done in that largeness of frame and minutiae of detail that she later analyzes in the work of

Rembrandt. She has painted her biblical scenes with words as he did them with pigments, somber and vivid at once; dramatic and massive in composition. The book traces a long, subtly modulated progression from the sensuous, bragging, faintly corrupt shepherd boy to the aged, dying King of Israel, exhausted by the journey of the flesh and his grapplings with Jahveh. In its impressive gallery, the second figure is that of the tormented, tragic Saul. Miss Schmitt's ability to capture ambivalence is at its most subtle and complex in this book, not only in the strains of emotion and mingled motive between David and Saul, but within every set of relationships.

We could say that Gladys Schmitt's modern novels are composed in a minor key and the historical ones in a major key. Yet in all the major works, but especially in *David*, the minor strain is present. It wanders like the thin reed voice of oboes through the quiet figurations and counterpoints between the smashing crescendos of her heavy orchestration. It is heard, for instance, in the relations between David and Jonathan, the son of Saul; between David and Michal, the daughter of Saul; and between David and Achish, the Philistine lord of Gath.

Many aspects of love enter the life of David. There is the unmistakably erotic bond between himself and Jonathan, "passing the love of women." It is of some interest to our age that both of these men sense that for them there is no consummation save death. There are both yearning and discipline, a combination not often seen in our literature: ". . . the ancient admonition, the old, unalterable law came between them." But on his deathbed, David perceives what touches not only Jonathan but many other relationships of mankind, that "for those who put off the flesh, there are no interdictions against love."

But the flesh is not slighted. There is a gamut in David's life involving such variations of passion and hunger as those he felt for Michal, partly but not wholly a surrogate for her brother; the child Ahinoam, whose patient lot closes bitterly; the lush Bathsheba and, at the end, the little Shunamite, Abishag, who in bed was only bodily warmth to him, but in comfort was so much more. With Ahinoam, called Noi, and with Abishag, Miss Schmitt deals with a tenderness that she has matched perhaps only in the bond between Rembrandt and his father, and between the painter and his own dying son, Titus.

Between Saul and David a tormenting tension of devotion and mutual suspicion lies. It is an anguish to the king, contributing to his lapses into madness. Saul, David, the prophet Samuel and Jahveh are involved in an intricate quartet. Insofar as obedience is love, David has loved his implacable God too, and the tenderness mingled in this often bitter bond is shown in the songs of worship and in David's ecstatic dance before the Ark of the Covenant. My only reservation is a feeling that we do not quite see the aspect of the fully mature psalmist.

The tensions and ambivalences of a father's love are seen in relation to the several sons: Amnon, Adonijah, Absalom and Solomon, of his own flesh, and even in his feelings for Meribaal, son of Jonathan.

In his meditations, the aged David concludes about these diverse relationships: "I loved them all, and the love wherewith I loved them was the same love."

In the smaller frame of her next novel, *Alexandra*, this unity at the heart of love is echoed in a girl's voice, speaking of many loves: "The same, really. All of them a sort of reflection, like light in a mirror, and all the same."

Another emotion is harbored by old David, the love of remembered trifles, which has an affinity with Thornton Wilder's "value above all price for the smallest events in our daily life." For David it becomes crystallized in a remembered fig tree, the sound of his father's hammer, bread hot from the hearth, and his mother's hand upon the loom.

Even in the weakest of Miss Schmitt's novels, *The Persistent Image*, in which the hero is shrunk to the scale of a dyspeptic record-shop owner in mediocre patterns of life, a truth about love lies at the core, deserving a better embodiment. He is incapable of self-transcending love because the child of his beloved is to him a "persistent image" of her previous husband. He breaks these neurotic shackles when the sudden necessity to act for the protection of the child forces him to see her as a person, freeing him to love both the child and her mother.

Gladys Schmitt is, in a special sense, an artist's artist, for the creative processes in several of the arts are an absorbing preoccupation with her. She has remarked that bodies are less permanent than their images in art. She captures that magical transmutation by which the objects of life are reassembled in art, as Rembrandt transmuted faces of his simple family into saints and kings. Ellie Hasselman is a painter and we believe in her ability. Alexandra, in the novel that bears her name, is a gifted actress. *A Small Fire* is about the world of music, its narrator a singer and the other leading figure a pianist. A love for and wide acquaintance with music is reflected in everything Miss Schmitt writes. Her concern with painting and with the processes of the artist reaches its culmination in *Rembrandt*.

She knows the discipline of the arts and that self-indulgence is a fatal pitfall in any of them. The most interesting aspects of *A Small Fire* are not in the rather tense story and characterizations, but in the reflections of the teaching processes in a music school. Here she analyzes the techniques of the art and stresses its rigors and austerities.

In *Alexandra* we are shown, flamboyantly but validly, a similar rigor applied to teaching the art of acting, especially in a sequence in which Alexandra is being coached in Cordelia's lines in the fourth act of *Lear*. The artist's temperament, that essential element so often at war with the required discipline, is well remarked in a comment about the young actress:

> It was not that she lied, or even exaggerated . . . it was only that, in every significant moment of her life, she sounded the heights and the depths before she found her bearings on the world.

The young David is asked by Saul about his songs, "Which came first . . . the music or the poem?" He replies, "They come separately and yet they come together. A little of this calls up a little of that, and so it goes." In this simplicity is summed up much of the art of composition in whatever medium.

Rembrandt searches these questions exhaustively. As a novel of the work and growth of an artist it merits comparison with the high points of *Jean-Christophe* while, at the same time, it is not marked by the unevennesses that mar Rolland's masterwork. I am forced to neglect here how memorably it evokes the man, his family, his circle and his times. Enough to say that it reaches an exaltation and purgation, in the struggles of both art and life, to make one weep. Indeed, Miss Schmitt displays this same high tear-evoking capacity in *David* and *Confessors* as well. It comes from the loftiest responses and is at an utter remove from shallow sentimentality.

Early the young Rembrandt defines the learning process:

. . . there was little enough to be learned from a master beyond the basic skills . . . a person learned the best and the most of it alone, by cleansing his eyes of every borrowed image and by looking without hypocrisy and self-pity into the recesses of his own heart.

When asked by his friend Dr. Tulp, central figure of his first great *Anatomy Lesson*, why he wants to "stick human beings onto canvas," he replies, ". . . the very act of painting them becomes the best way of seeing them. . . ." Years later he realizes that

it was only in the act of painting—not in meditation, not in converse with his fellows, not even in the act of love—that he could break open the fruit of life and know its ultimate sweetness.

What better insight can we find into the dry periods of an artist's life than is expressed in Rembrandt's sense, at one time, of "painting with increasing mastery and decreasing involvement."

As the novel gathers toward its close we see the strains that motivate the man, "great in his art and great in his spirit," impelled by "the passion, the rage, the grief, the fierce and uncontrollable need to search and to know. . . ." It was not fashions, fads, or favor of patrons, but rather "God and the great dead against whom he had measured himself all his days. . . ." The self-portraits that absorbed him more and more in his declining years were the means of unsparing self-examination. He has learned that "to be human is to suffer bereavement, agony, and death"; that "whatever blunders we made, we can't erase them—we've got to absorb them somehow into the stuff of our lives."

This dying man:

> What had he hoped for then? More than he had gotten? No, it was only that what he had gotten was more exalted and more terrible, different only as that which was wrought by destiny or the hand of God was different from what men, poor artificers that they were, fashioned vainly and shallowly in their waking dreams.

He had articulated it early—the nature of the artist's creative process, be it composing, painting, writing: "a struggle between Jacob and the angel." To be great it can be nothing less.

There is not, in Gladys Schmitt's books, an overt commitment to any creed. But there is a profound and brooding sense of God and a vision of man as created and endowed by Him. She has also a deep comprehension of committed lives, both in the Old Testament and New Testament contexts.

The whole of *David the King* is enacted under the shadow of Jahveh. The biblical frame is cruelly large in its demands. It engulfs all who come to it with anything cheaper than its mighty concepts and try to use its narrative frame as a mere outline. But it yields inexhaustible riches to those who will grapple with it, as Jacob with the angel. Gladys Schmitt is such a one. She grasps fully the essence of the Old Testament epic of the houses of Saul and David, which William G. Pollard and Robert Pfeiffer have called *The Hebrew Iliad* in an excellent translation and annotation of the earliest texts of that chronicle.

There is powerful force in the attempt of the sinful servant of Jahveh to repent his murder of Uriah the Hittite. For a long time, like the king in *Hamlet*, he cannot make his words go up. For days he wrestled in agony with this word "repent"; "O God, whom I earnestly seek to know, I bitterly repent . . ." until "the husk of the word was broken at last, so that its essence was poured forth upon him, and he bowed his head upon his knees and wept." And the dying King David reflects:

> I have done much evil all my days, but this at least may be said of me—that I knew evil, even when I had done it with my own hands.

I think there is a minor flaw when David, struggling against "the ulcer of meaninglessness" at the core of his spirit, concludes that God sees him not, sees no man, does not look upon the world. I think this is a concept not possible in Old Testament Israel, although it was common for Israel to defy or reproach God. But the dying David urges his spirit, rendering it up eagerly to "that Everlasting Being from whom we issued forth and unto whom we go at last."

In *Confessors of the Name* Miss Schmitt gives her

major expression to man's encounter with God in dedication and sacrifice. This is a richly textured canvas of third-century Rome. No small part of its achievement is that the Emperor Decius, the austere virtuous pagan, launching the persecution as part of a futile effort to check the decay of Roman society, is himself movingly, understandingly painted.

His nephew Favorinus, a Stoic, has reached the classical preconditions for conversion. He is haunted by a sense of responsibility for the world he did not make. He yearns, like the Marquesa de Montemayor, in Wilder's *Bridge of San Luis Rey*, for evidence of some "sane, just Force." He cannot accept a world of blind chance: "I reject it, I would rather be a heap of senseless ashes than live my life in such a world." At the end of a long road Favorinus still is a reserved convert, but he confesses the Name and goes to the crimson confession of martyrdom. If he is not unreservedly committed to what the Name is, he has rejected firmly all that is not the Name and he has brought fresh morale to the last band of Christians to die under the Decian persecution.

The picture of the early Church is absorbing and honest. It is especially interesting if one looks back at a secularist's interpretation of that Church offered by Professor Maurer in *The Gates of Aulis*. Possibly no single scene Miss Schmitt has written is more difficult to bring off or more triumphantly purging in its capture of ultimate dedication than the description of Favorinus's cousin Paulina going, with sixty other

Christians, to the lions in the Flavian amphitheatre. Here she has caught nobility. An atheist denying the reality of the faith could not deny the majesty of the act.

But not all are called to martyrdom or capable of it. She examines the dilemma of the lapsed Christians, those whose courage failed and who burned the incense on the pagan altars as required by law. The Elder Novatian was adamant about these: they must be excommunicated. The Elder Cornelius and the martyred Elder Moyses, one of her most moving portraits, disagreed. Novatian, the ecstatic mystic, had forgotten Peter's denial of his Lord. It is Moyses, tortured and near painful death, who sends from prison the word:

> Be gracious and forgiving, according to the spirit and the letter of our Redeemer, who died to save sinners. Let the lost sheep, who in their fright and in their childishness burned incense before the daemons, be freely forgiven. Appoint for them a proper period of penance, and let them return thereafter to free-hearted fellowship with their brothers and sisters in Christ. Also to alms and prayers and the breaking of bread.

Miss Schmitt later shows us Rembrandt van Rijn seeking models for the face of Jesus not among his friends, the rich and cultured Sephardic Jews from Spain, but among the gaunt and fiercely orthodox Ashkenazim, refugees from Poland. So, in large images and small, she weaves into a web her skeins of multifaceted human love, revealing the ways of those most alive of all men—creative and believing men—and their wrestlings with the angel and with God.

She has the classical perception of nobility, that attribute that, before any flaw is discerned, is necessary to make tragedy possible. It permeates all her historical books. The modern ones reveal rather that our framework and vision are shrunken, contracted, collapsed upon themselves. What we see there are evidences of the loss, the sometime groping for nobility, the hunger for it and the anxious uncertainty that it is possible.

Miss Schmitt's whole will and striving in all her books is toward affirmation of man's dignity and personal uniqueness as the flawed image of God. She never goes by cheap ways or uses that easy affirmation that is sentimentality. She knows that the price of grandeur is paid in anguish.

Alan Paton: tragedy and beyond

Much has been published recently about the decline of tragedy, and the question has been asked whether tragedy can be written in this age. Offstage, during the discussion, Alan Paton went ahead and did it—in terms of the novel—in *Too Late the Phalerope*. It was the book that followed his much-acclaimed first novel, *Cry, the Beloved Country*. It offered him, therefore, all the notorious "second book" challenges, as well as the problems of tragedy. The two books are an interesting study in the tragic —and an element beyond. For the purposes of this discussion, I will reverse the order in which they were written.

The core of *Too Late the Phalerope* is classically simple: Pieter van Vlanderen, a police lieutenant, honored in the community, breaks the iron law of the South African Immorality Act. Thereby he is destroyed and his family with him. A secret flaw has brought about the fall of a man of stature. He comprehends what has happened, and recognizes his own responsibility in it. Nevertheless, the story contains forces that become cumulative inevitabilities, helping to thrust him on an inexorable path. As in *Cry, the Beloved Country*, we are given a balanced picture of environmental influences coexistent with personal responsibility.

Four major factors—two of which are social and two, personal—produce the tragedy. The first of these is the psychotic rigidity of the Afrikaner community in South Africa. An illicit sexual encounter might cause varying degrees of trouble in marriage, family, and community anywhere. But it is not sex that destroys Pieter—it is race. Even in his puritanical environment, the shock of a misstep with a white woman could have been absorbed. But by sexual contact with a black woman, Pieter has violated taboo, far more formidable than statutory law, though in this case a law gives formal expression to the taboo. An irrational horror, a sense of ritual uncleanness, attaches to the offense. Within that community, he can never be cleansed. His name is destroyed irreparably and all who bear his name are consumed in the shame of it.

The second social element is puritanism, in the community and in Pieter's father, Jacob van Vlanderen. The puritanism of the community, of course, has theological and historical roots that predate the race psychosis. But there has been a natural, inevitable absorption of the one strain into the other, so that they have become indissoluble and mutually reinforcing. Thus a deep emotional disturbance has been given the sanction of morality and the prejudice of man translated into the law of God.

It is such men as Jacob van Vlanderen who make up the Afrikaner community, and it is partly the community that has formed Jacob van Vlanderen, putting its own stamp upon those elements of character that are uniquely his. He is a good man in the letter of the law and of puritan moral codes, but praise of him, if such it be, must stop there. He is as hard and merciless a judge of men as any who ever walked in the line of Calvin and Knox in colonial America or puritan England.

The unyielding will and emotional insensitivity of Jacob are the root of the first of the personal disorders that prepare the long way for Pieter's fall: a deep hostility between father and son. In the boy's childhood, the father had honored only the hard, masculine side of a more complex nature. He had trodden roughly on the sensitive or intellectual elements of his son—the qualities derived from his mother and responsive to her gentleness. Indeed, the mother has largely been compelled, through her husband's hardness, to cede the boy to the hungry maternal love (and ambiguously more) of Jacob's sister, Tante Sophie, the hare-lipped spinster who is the elegiac narrator of the tale.

Tante Sophie, who frankly calls herself a "watcher," tells the tale in a generally direct way, though the limits of knowledge in first-person narration are occasionally strained, in spite of the device of a secret journal of Pieter's, from which she quotes in retrospect. In recurring passages of high rhapsodic tone—definitely conventionalized—she functions as chorus. It is both effective and slightly overdone. In the classic tragic manner, she reiterates the already accomplished doom, so that the suspense, which is great, is not the suspense of "whether" but the greater one of "how."

The tensions between father and son flared up over the Second World War, when Pieter enlisted for what Jacob called an "English war." The two are opposed on every major question in life, including attitude toward the race question and the notion of what religion should be. The father never gives up trying to assert over Pieter the utter dominance he wields over the rest of the family. Yet he and Pieter grope vainly for some bond between them.

The fourth of the major destructive factors is the tension between Pieter and his wife, Nella. She is of a gentle and timorous nature, loving her husband but unable to venture into the depths of his mind and spirit where his dangerous conflicts rage. Also there is an inhibition upon their sexual life. Puritanism has conditioned Nella to believe in a sharp division between the bodily passions and the other elements of love, which in her eyes are essentially "higher." She gives herself and then withdraws. Pieter longs for a sustained sexual harmony with her, based on an acceptance of the unity of all aspects of love. Failure to achieve this does contribute to Pieter's *swartgalligheid*, the deadly black mood, but we shall examine whether this whole factor is as crucial as he believes it to be—or in the way he thinks it is.

I have not cited Tante Sophie as a factor in the disaster, though she regards herself as one. She is not causative, but may have failed to be preventive. Whether or not if she had "cried out not ceasing" she could have averted the catastrophe is unprovable. It belongs among all the other *ifs* that tantalize hindsight.

I put aside also the active malice of Sergeant Steyn, Pieter's subordinate who betrays him, for it is a by-product of Pieter's tensions and is a circumstantial factor. Pieter was courting exposure unconsciously—if not by one, then by another.

The obsessive drive that carries Pieter to the secretly-smiling black girl, Stephanie, takes its rise from a constellation of factors which I would not presume to analyze clinically. Paton has captured the agony of obsession powerfully. But sex surely is more the operational means than the aim of it. A game of symbol-hunting might be played with the image of the bird and the name of the bird that is the occasion of a fleeting communication between this father and son. On the face of it, however, Paton, by his emphasis, has given this relationship the crucial place. He suggests that if some bond of emotion and

interest had really united these two, in Pieter's boyhood, the tragedy would not have happened. The
search for the phalerope, with its flash of grace,
comes too late; ironically, it is after Pieter is already
fatally entangled.

A bitter, buried core of hostility is the explosive
charge in Pieter. It takes its shattering force from
the thick, hard casing of the social environment
which provides the containing pressure that makes
all great explosions. The immediate fuse is the sexual
strain with Nella.

But Pieter is confused in his sense of this. He
pleads obliquely to Nella about the "safety" in her
love.

> . . . if you could love me more often, I'd be safe,
> I said. . . .
> —Safe? Against what, Pieter?
> —Against anything, my love. Against fear and
> danger. And the black moods.
> I wanted to say against temptation, I wanted to
> say against the thing that tempts me, the thing I
> hate; I wanted to tell her every word, to strip my-
> self naked before her, so that she could see the
> nature of the man she loved, with all his fears and
> torments, and be filled by it with such compassion
> as would heal and hold him for ever.

Tante Sophie is mistaken on this point, too. She
remarks:

> For have I not seen a score of times with my eyes,
> when men and women are denied, how they go
> seeking? Like a man who is robbed of a jewel, and

goes seeking it amongst the dross and filth, and all men look on him with pity and contempt, not knowing of his distress.

The observation has truth in it, but is not as applicable to Pieter as he and she believe.

If it were simply consuming sexual hunger driving Pieter he could and would have found means to appease it, secretly and safely, within his own race. But "the thing that he hates," this "something that could bring no joy," is not only sexual, with the piquancy of a primitive, raw lust, it is also destruction and revenge. This is the one sure and deadly blow against his father, against Nella and his children, against Tante Sophie, and against the Afrikaner community. To this should be added—and against himself. These are his hates. He does not comprehend them; his real motivation is well below the level of his consciousness. He does not understand that he loves and hates at the same time.

Tante Sophie, interpreting him partly from his own journal, has him tormenting himself with the question, "What kind of man would destroy what he had created, and hurt what he had loved?" But this is the symbolic enigma of Euripides' *The Madness of Herakles*. It is the tortured refrain of Oscar Wilde, in "The Ballad of Reading Gaol":

For each man kills the thing he loves. . . .

In Wilde, the generalization is romantically, indulgently exaggerated and facile—but there is a seed of

truth, and that seed is what sprouts in the heart of
Pieter van Vlanderen.

His ambivalence toward Nella (and their children
are, in this context, an extension of her) springs from
frustration and confinement. Her gentleness exists
within the communal harshness and is conditioned
by it. At the beginning of the book, Pieter lets off
with a warning the boy, Dick, who was pursuing
that same Stephanie with whom Pieter is to become
entangled. He warns the boy that conviction may be
a year, two years—"But outside it's a sentence for
life."

When Pieter confides the episode to Nella she
says first,

> . . . to think he was in this house.

Then:

> . . . you forgave him.
> —Yes.
> —I'll not forgive him.

Pieter cannot reach her in complete unity, sexu-
ally, because of her deep-grained puritan condition-
ing, though she loves him and tries. But that is not a
total impasse and is not enough to drive him to the
black girl. The basic trouble is, he cannot communicate his whole nature to Nella as he desperately needs
to do. For expressing and exploring his rebellion
against the communal code, her softness is as im-
permeable as his father's hardness. Ironically, only

to the cloying, smothering, self-tormenting Tante Sophie, whose love for him has more of a buried sexual tinge than she can bear to face, could Pieter have communicated his whole heart and mind. For while she is a disquieting and faintly repellent woman, she is nonetheless a remarkable one. There is one scene of cruel laceration between herself and Pieter when he lashes savagely at her smothering possessiveness, the quality that hopelessly nullifies the possibility of a saving communication between them. "In God's name, have you no pride?" She recoils into her shame "that a man should think me a woman to whom such words could be spoken."

Pieter is driven by rebellious resentment against a total community that confines him everywhere, and crowns the injury by idolizing him as an athlete. He is forced to be what they will have him be. Jacob is the archetypal figure of the community; in him, Pieter can focus both the communal and the filial resentments. In loving them all and hating them all, the one sure, irrevocable blow he can strike against them and his hated self, is the breaking of the racial-sexual taboo.

He is not sophisticated in matters of deep psychic cleavages. As the darkness and light struggle in him, he thinks only vaguely and remotely—and that too late—of going to Johannesburg, to "see one of those psychiatrists, who might tell him some secret of salvation. . . ." There is no priest who can help him, in this puritan church. So he looks among his learned books [Paton is disappointingly vague about *what* books]

> that told all the sins and weaknesses of men, hoping
> to find himself . . . he read there of the misery of
> other men's lives, and the dark crimes and sins that
> they committed, and he did not know if they were
> sinning, or asking, and knocking at strange and
> terrible doors. And he found himself in a sad tor-
> mented company, and had pity for all twisted souls,
> and most for himself that found himself with them.

Inevitably, comparisons with *The Scarlet Letter* and *Crime and Punishment* arise. Once Pieter has committed his act, there is no possible release for him but total exposure—a dilemma he shares in part with Arthur Dimmesdale and Raskolnikov. Paton gives us a long sequence of superb suspense, arising out of guilty misunderstandings of innocent natural coincidences. But just as the death wish is commonly unconscious, so Pieter suffers an agonized dread of discovery, unconscious of the fact that it is that exposure and its consequences that have motivated him from the start.

This, it seems to me, is what Paton has wrought intuitively. It is not made wholly clear to any of the persons in the book and it is not possible to say how far it was present in Paton's conscious intention, but it is at least intuitively unerring in all the elements as presented.

Paton remains unswervingly honest in his resolutions. Jacob's implacable striking out of Pieter's name from the very book of life, and his embittered death, are the inevitable course of his nature. The savage lines of the 9th Psalm, that the old man reads in a ritual of casting off, are ambiguous, for in them he indicts the son, and we indict the father.

Tante Sophie goes keening down the wind. No easy claim is made for Nella's and Pieter's future. The sentence was for life, in the sense in which he had warned Dick. We know that Pieter and Nella could go away from that rigid country to start again, after he leaves prison, but we do not know that they will. We know that Nella could be changed by Pieter's secret journal, but we do not know if she will.

What we know concretely are a number of responses to the facts. Sergeant Steyn disappears, a necessary Judas somehow trapped in this role as his great prototype had been. The young policeman, Vorster, to whom Pieter had shown much kindness and who had hero-worshipped him, turns to rend him. Pieter's mother, as always, is mutely wounded, though loving. His sister withdraws from her betrothal in an access of shame. Kappie, the Jew, remains perceptively loyal, grieving that he could not have averted his friend's disaster. Nella's father is only a slightly less overpowering equivalent of Jacob.

The great responses, which bring the book to its final dimensions, are those of the English police captain and Tante Sophie. It is the captain who says to

Sophie, in lines that touch the person, in Jacob, and also the community and the state:

> . . . an offender must be punished, *mejuffrou*, I don't argue about that. But to punish and not to restore, that is the greatest of all offenses.
> —Is that the sin against the Holy Ghost? I said.
> —I don't know, he said, but I hope not, for I once committed it.
> And I dared to say to him, was that your son?
> —Yes, he said. Yes, it was my son. But I am resolved never again to commit it.

When Nella's father says fiercely that he would shoot Pieter like a dog, because "he has offended against the race," the captain replies:

> . . . as a policeman I know an offense against the law, and as a Christian I know an offense against God; but I do not know an offense against the race.

The tragedy is complete, with its full purgation through pity and terror. If something arises after it, for Pieter and Nella, that will be another story, as Dostoyevsky remarks of Raskolnikov's future at the end of *Crime and Punishment*.

Cry, the Beloved Country is tragic, but is not a tragedy in the formal literary sense, and it carries the clear affirmation of an element transcending the tragic view of life. This element is Christian, but it is not only in Christianity that such transcendence of tragedy is possible. That most tightly implacable of

the Greek tragedies, *Oedipus Tyrannus,* is followed
by the mystical transcendence of *Oedipus at Colon-
nus.* Again in a Christian frame, there are transcendent elements at the close of *The Brothers Karamazov*
which would have come to flower in the projected
further novel about Alyosha which Dostoyevsky did
not live to write.

In *Cry, the Beloved Country* the primary story is
pathetic, in that the suffering characters are more
bewildered victims than prime movers in their difficulties. The tragic elements are social, and as always, complexly interlocked in cause and effect.
The destruction of the soil, the breaking of the tribal
system and the home, the tight segregation of South
African society producing ghetto slums, the com-
pound system in the mines, the provocative juxtapo-
sition of the haves and the have-nots: these are the
specific and local social factors working upon the
general and universal human nature. The story is fiction, but Paton says in an Author's Note, "as a social
record it is the plain and simple truth."

The shock effects of a cultural frontier are not
unique to Africa. Interesting parallel elements can
be seen in Oliver LaFarge's *Laughing Boy,* in terms
of the American Indians. When any tribal system is
shattered by the white man, but the tribal people are
not taken into the white man's culture, deterioration
and tragedy are inevitable. The African priest Msi-
mangu, in Johannesburg, one of the compelling figures of the book, says,

The tragedy is not that things are broken. The tragedy is that they are not mended again. The white man has broken the tribe. And it is my belief . . . that it cannot be mended again.

Cry, the Beloved Country is a splendid piece of craftsmanship, extraordinary as a first book by a man in middle life, whose work had been in education and penology. The most jaded reviewers were won by the fresh, individual lyricism of its style and the passion of its conviction and its thirst for justice. Paton's use of idioms and rhythms from Zulu, Bantu, Xosa and Afrikaans speech contributed greatly to the fresh effect. Now that his work is well known, and now that other writers have used these language patterns, Paton's style still has its personal stamp, and we must not let familiarity dull our recollection of its first invigorating impact.

The book is skillfully constructed in parallels. The simple African Anglican priest, Stephen Kumalo, loses his son, Absalom. The African-English farmer, James Jarvis, loses his son, Arthur. It is Absalom who kills Arthur, for which the state kills Absalom.

By the keenest of the ironies in which the book is rich, Arthur Jarvis was among the greatest friends of the black man, in the forefront of the struggle for justice. The senseless tragedy that links the two sons ultimately links the two fathers. There is no finer scene in a consistently moving book than that in which Stephen Kumalo and James Jarvis first come face to face, by chance, after the shooting, and realize one another's identities.

The ramifications of the story are comprehensive, showing the life of the tribal country and of the city. Through Stephen's journey to Johannesburg to search for his sister and his son, we see how that city, with its mine compounds and shantytown slums, swallows up people and breeds criminals. The quest involves a vivid tour of the native districts, and of the reformatory of which Paton himself had been superintendent. In interpolated meditations on the courts, and upon a new gold field, he deepens the social texture. Most adroit touch of all: the papers and speeches and books of the dead Arthur Jarvis are made the medium of direct polemical statement, and also of growth in the character of James Jarvis.

The father had not approved or understood his son's position on the race question. One could have imagined an implacable hardening on the issue after the tragedy, as would have been found in a temperament like Jacob van Vlanderen's: "I always told him he was a fool—and now one of the so-and-so's has shot him!" Instead, the grace that gradually works in James Jarvis is that of love, for he had loved the young man, even without comprehending him. When he is exposed to his son's papers, in the solitude of grief, he finds him for the first time and perceives that to repudiate his son's principles now will be truly to lose him utterly. By honoring and carrying forward his son's actions, something is retained that cannot be lost even in death. It is a measure both of the man, and of the remedial power of love. The new James Jarvis is "a man who put his feet upon a road, and . . . no man would turn him from it."

Among the central threads of the book is the question of Stephen Kumalo's response to his son's guilt, as contrasted to the attitude of his politician-brother, John Kumalo, toward his own son's involvement as an accessory in the shooting.

John Kumalo, whose experience of the city has led him to cast off the faith, is solely concerned with evading punishment for his son and trouble for himself. He is aware that the boy was present, but is successful in obtaining his acquittal through perjury. In John's terms, he has been successful, but we expect that the last state will be worse than the first. The prospects are not bright for his son.

Stephen, on the other hand, faces a profound discovery. Once his son's guilt is established, it is impossible for him, as a Christian, to seek to evade punishment. His most urgent concern is for his son's repentance. He sees that Absalom, whose name, "his father's peace," is as ironic for Kumalo as it had been for King David, is more unhappy that he has been caught than for what he has done. To lead the boy to repentance becomes his first aim. For the Christian, ultimate welfare is not a question of the life or death of the body, but the life or death of the soul.

Repentance is validated by the acceptance of punishment. After the confessed guilt, after the accepted punishment, then mercy (in men's terms) may or may not be forthcoming. But mercy is not to be given on sentimental impulse. Mercy follows judgment; it does not precede it.

John Kumalo would save his son's life and does not believe in his soul. Stephen would be grateful for his son's life, but would not wish it bartered for his soul. At the end, there is hope for Absalom's repentance—though only God can judge of it.

Gertrude, Stephen's sister, whose degraded state had been the direct cause of Stephen's summons to Johannesburg, is lost. She has gone beyond her personal point of return. The effort of self-examination and rehabilitation is more than she can sustain. She slips away, just before the return of the little party of family survivors to the home village of Ndotsheni.

Yet there is salvage from the loss and pain. It is this that leads Paton beyond tragedy and that prompts the subtitle of the book: "A Story of Comfort in Desolation." If Absalom has repented, he has not lost both life and soul, as he had been in the way to do. Carried back to Ndotsheni (the account of their arrival is a magnificent lyrical passage), from the certainty of loss in Johannesburg to the possibility of new life, are Gertrude's son, Absalom's wife, and her unborn child. Stephen Kumalo and James Jarvis are enlarged in spirit, and from the spirit come works that promise the renewal of the land around Ndotsheni.

•   •   •

No voice out of South Africa has been so eloquent, so passionately just, with a social morality so deeply grounded in a religious premise. Granted Paton's fine gifts, his work also demonstrates the opportunity offered the writer in a place and time of acute moral and social crisis.

His books have flowed from humane indignation, anxiety, and the desire for reform. They are a patriot's books, for South Africa, in which he is so much a minority voice, is indeed, to him, the beloved country. What further work we may expect from him, who has given us so much in the two novels, depends partly on events in South Africa. Both novels were written outside the country, for he has found the internal pressure and involvement too great for sustained work there. Yet these were the fruit of separate and relatively short absences, for he steadfastly refuses to become an expatriate.

At this present writing, his passport has been taken from him, following his brief visit to the United States in the fall of 1960, to accept an award from Freedom House. Until it is restored, he cannot leave the country without incurring exile. The volume of stories and sketches published in 1960 as *Tales from a Troubled Land* (in England, *Debbie Go Home*), reflects his problem of working in the midst of his direct political involvements, such as his post as president of the Liberal Party of South Africa.

These tales are interesting, sometimes moving. The best group is those which directly relate events during his administration of Diepkloof Reformatory. They show the appalling problems in the path of the native in Johannesburg. They would be worth re-working, with additional material, into a complete book about this extraordinary experience, whether presented as fiction or memoir. The most powerful and terrifying of the other stories, in which some of the force and cadence of the novels appears, is "Life for a Life," which describes the events after the killing of an Afrikaner farmer. In sum, the stories have an importance because Alan Paton wrote them. They would not have made Alan Paton important as the novels did.

Thus one of the most intensely individual literary talents of our day stands perhaps temporarily silenced, in the strife-torn land that gave him his great themes. From his experience in the beloved country there may yet come other major works. There could always come personal tragedy. The measure of his books is that while distilling the essence of South Africa, they speak to many aspects of the condition of the whole world. He has struck universal notes, and the world outside his own land honors him for his art, his humanity, and his integrity.

C. P. Snow: spokesman of two communities

C. P. Snow is the nearest approach to a Balzac in modern England. The comparison is not made simply for the obvious reason that he has written a large series of interlocking books with recurring characters. Other writers have done so with good and bad results. We may admire the ambition and energy, but no merit automatically accrues to the effort. Like Balzac, Snow is zestfully interested in the technical details of a variety of professions and walks of life. He is absorbed by the whole texture of a culture and a period. He presents us with views of several levels of society with keen observation of their characteristics and typical modes of operation. He shows us the intricate hierarchies in university life, science, some facets of the law, and the functioning of the British civil service from the ministerial level downward. These aspects of Snow's work justify the analogy, although his spread is not so broad; he does not reach as far as the outermost fringes of Balzac's inclusiveness. As an Englishman, he lacks the Gallic sensuousness, the erotic coloration, also the occasional sheer melodramatic nonsense which are found in Balzac.

Justice Oliver Wendell Holmes, who was criticized as coldly intellectual in his approach to the law, protested, "To think is not less than to feel." It is fair to call Snow's novels more cerebral and objective than emotional. Yet all are narrated in the first person, an essentially subjective device, used by many nowadays for sheer orgies of solipsism. Snow *does* feel as well as think. There are tides of deep emotion in the novels. He has a particular gift for depicting the subtler, contained emotions (some might say disciplined; others, repressed) of people of education, cultivation and sensitivity, who live, work and express themselves more through the mind and through words than through the senses or dramatic physical action. In a period when the senses dominate fiction, when many writers deliberately abdicate reason, he is prominent among the select group who are artists with their minds and not just with their emotions, muscles, or glands. He gives us intelligent people pursuing rational and purposeful lives, withal as muddled and misguided at times as is the way of the race. He can *think* a novel as well as feel one. As a corollary to this, he is not related to the cult of youth or eternal adolescence, but can begin a characterization in boyhood and carry it through to seasoned maturity.

What Snow arouses from us in each book is an intense interest in its development, amounting in the best of them to a fascination. Cumulatively, it becomes a deep absorption in the whole pattern of his world. What is not found, even when we are genuinely moved, is the experience of purgation through pity or terror. This is not the commodity in which he deals. His novels can be called absorbing, but we would not call them powerful in their emotional impact.

Snow is a conventional, traditional novelist in form and style—a perceiver, not an innovator. An addiction to old-fashioned chapter titles is a tacit and charming acknowledgment of this. His style is unobtrusive and lucid—also unpretentious—the vehicle for his thought, not his personality. But it has an epigrammatic wit that flashes often, as in his description of a certain literary journalist, broadcaster, adviser—rather than writer—as "high up in the civil service of literature." He has particular skill in dialogue, freeing it deftly from burdensome identification of speakers, summarizing where it need not be spun out, and letting it flow as a playwright would do. His other chief technical quality is a large architectural sense. He builds most of the novels well as independent entities, and they are organized and overlapped with high skill in the series plan.

But our interest remains in what he is telling and

showing us, rather than in his means. He is a realist whose concept of reality means a broad vision and a long perspective on social and individual behavior, not the minutiae of abnormal psychology or fringe-society. The refreshing element in his books is the sense of a large, varied and effectively functioning world peopled by all sorts and conditions of men. Its focus is within the central bands of the spectrum. He does not preoccupy himself with the warped and distorted, although personal and social warps and distortions are encountered in his world. Balance is one of his most marked characteristics.

His well-known lectures show, along with the novels, that Snow is a concerned and worried man, fully aware—indeed, as a scientist, among the first to be aware—of the threat to our survival. But he stands apart from the reactions of panic and despair, or the philosophies of meaninglessness. He depicts a world of meaningful and purposeful action in which men are affected by the chaotic elements in their time but need not inevitably be engulfed by or surrender to them. It is a world of pressures, principalities, and powers, but one which still has enough open options to challenge a man and to permit response.

In religious matters he is a skeptic but not an arrogant denier. He does not believe, but he respects belief. It is not a force in his life, but he recognizes its force in other lives. He knows the historical relationship of Western religious belief to the ethical and intellectual patterns of the unbeliever—that faith formed the ethos from which some have expelled it. Himself a liberal, speculative, humanistic moralist, he is, like his narrator Lewis Eliot, "careful about others' faith." Also like him, he has a certain note of determinism, believing that we are each born with an essential nature that we cannot change.

A great many non-believing writers have lost touch so utterly with the believing community as to have fallen into the notion that it no longer exists. A gap has opened, of which they are not even aware, in their view of the life and behavior around them. Their moral sense, if exercised at all, is in a curious vacuum or else eccentrically private. Their image of religious belief, if they try to imagine it, is a ludicrous distortion. Snow the skeptic is quite free of these flaws.

Snow is a contrast to Lawrence Durrell, whose vogue also is flourishing. In the Alexandria Quartet, Durrell tells the same story four times over, from different perspectives. The world of these books is exotic and decadent. Virtuosity of style is a primary element in their appeal. Essentially the quartet is a *tour de force.* There is realistic observation in it, but there is also a substantial measure of high-level hokum and sensation-seeking. It plays for effect. The sense of performance, of watching wheels go round, is ever present. Reflection on the quartet reveals less matter and more art than otherwise.

Snow covers the same ground, or overlaps, many times in his novels, not through different eyes, but

with different points of attention among simultaneous patterns of events. In a larger frame than Durrell's, he shows us many facets of places, institutions,
people and events. An impressive sense of reality in
stereopticon depth emerges as Snow retraces the
same period of elapsed time, with the same central
cast, as he does especially in *The Light and the Dark*,
The Masters, and a great part of *The New Men* and
Homecomings, and again in *Time of Hope*, *Strangers
and Brothers* and *The Conscience of the Rich*. His
virtual exclusion of the central subjects of each of
these books from the others—although they are obviously interrelated as to time, persons, and scene—
effectively shows how vastly much more there is to
tell of any life, character, or sequence of events than
any one or even several tellings can cover. Not
showily stylistic and exotically sensational like Durrell, Snow is incalculably more deeply, broadly, sol-
idly real as his narrator Lewis Eliot describes first one,
then another, and yet another of the overlapping experiences and observations in his orbit.

Power and Character

"I want a man who knows something about himself. And is appalled. And has to forgive himself to
get along."—Roy Calvert, in *The Masters*.

Few contemporary novelists would have written
those lines. I find in them a clue to Snow's whole sense
of character. They reflect the humanity and humility

which are constructively harnessed to a worldly knowingness and a shrewd judgment of men. In his Godkin Lectures, *Science and Government*, he mentions "people who are both cynical and unworldly, which is one of my least favorite combinations." He is himself the antithesis of such a blend. Tolerant of philosophy, faith, and foible, Snow as novelist can see all around a man, as one might walk around a Henry Moore sculpture, noting its holes and distortions, but also its proportions and solidities, its outlines as well as its emptinesses. He discloses, rather than exposes (a matter of attitude), what lies behind the façades of personality, and he does it with warmth, sometimes with regret.

Lewis Eliot is narrator of the entire *Strangers and Brothers* series. To what extent Eliot is an autobiographical figure is no one's business, but Eliot as the observer of life and character clearly speaks for Snow. *Time of Hope* and *Homecomings* are Eliot's books in that he is telling his own story as protagonist. It is this that makes them the most emotionally charged of all the books, with *The Light and the Dark* close behind them because of Lewis's bond with its central figure. Though he plays an important part in every other book, the center of the stage is held by another person, or by a group, for Snow is a particular master of ensemble drama.

In *Strangers and Brothers*, George Passant is central against the background of a midlands provincial town. In *The Conscience of the Rich* it is Charles

March, with a wealthy and powerful Jewish set of London as his background. *The Light and the Dark* is altogether Roy Calvert's book. *The Masters* and *The New Men* are extraordinary ensemble books, though Lewis's brother Martin can be called protagonist of the latter. *The Affair* (successfully dramatized for the London stage in 1961) is again distinctly an ensemble book, but one in which Lewis's role is so vital and central that it is also in a sense his.

Power is a constant theme of the novels. In chronology, its earliest note is heard in Lewis Eliot's boyhood ambitions in the midst of relative poverty:

> . . . I dreamed of fame—any kind of fame that would put my name in men's mouths, in the newspapers, make people recognize me in the streets. Sometimes I was a great politician, eloquent, powerful, venerated. Sometimes I was a writer as well known as Shaw. Sometimes I was extraordinarily rich. Always I had the power to make my own terms, to move through the world as one who owned it, to be waited on and give largesse.

The older Lewis Eliot frankly seeks and enjoys power, but well below the top echelons. Snow has not portrayed power at the highest levels of government. It may be partly because he has not moved on those lonely grounds, and his method pre-eminently is that of writing in detail about what he knows at first-hand. I think also it is because of the slightly Tolstoyan cast which he confesses in his historic vision.

In affairs of great moment, all is not, and cannot be, directed and brought to fruition from the top. He remarks in *Science and Government:*

> To get anything done in any highly articulated organization, you have got to carry people at all sorts of levels. It is their decisions, their acquiescence or enthusiasm (above all, the absence of their passive resistance), which are going to decide whether a strategy goes through in time.

It is especially this problem of power, unobtrusive, unpublicized, too often unrealized, but vital, that absorbs him.

In *The New Men* we get our closest view of power operating in government administration, specifically in the application of science to war. In *The Masters* we see the intense power struggle in the administration of a college at Cambridge. It is fascinating in itself, but is also a microcosm, a type of the political struggle anywhere.

There are several forms of the desire for power in the books, and three renunciations of it. Wealth is power. Charles March casts away the immediate advantage of his family's wealth by alienating himself from his father. He turns from the power potential which one with his connections would have found as a barrister, for a competent but obscure career in medicine. All this, Snow attributes to "the sick conscience of the rich" in "a bad generation into which to be born rich . . . If one had a talent for non-acceptance. . . ." This is an interesting point, but I think in using it as a title he makes too much of it. *The Conscience of the Rich* is a good novel, but is far more truly about tensions among the individuals in one family than about a social generalization of broad application, as implied in the title.

Still another of Snow's themes lies behind Charles's renunciation. Charles knows the temptation of cruelty. That is why he has escaped the channel of power prepared for him: "he had escaped from what he might do within it."

> When he spoke of wanting to lead a "useful" life . . . what he really meant was "good" . . . I sometimes thought it was those who were tempted to be cruel who most wanted to be good.

And much later:

> To know what goodness means, perhaps one needs to have lain awake at night, hating one's own nature.

This is in harmony with Roy Calvert's words about knowing oneself and being appalled.

In *The New Men*, Martin Eliot, Lewis's younger brother, feels the temptation of power when a major scientific administrative post comes within his grasp. He maneuvers ruthlessly for it, then, as if feeling that its possibilities for corruption have already begun to work in him, rejects it. Lewis reflects:

> It occurred to me that I had seen others make renunciations similar in kind to his: in each case they

gained happiness. It might have been otherwise, it might have been one of the ironies of the human condition that, when you throw away the game with a chance of winning it, you regret it ever after: but in the cases I had seen, it proved the contrary.

Lewis has made his own kind of renunciation. The needs, demands and drains upon him of his neurotic first wife, Sheila, forced him to step aside from his promising single-tracked career as barrister, unless he had chosen to sacrifice her to it, instead. His later reflections on Martin's action, the hard, long, but ultimately rewarding course his own life takes, make it clear that he does not resent or lament his choice. He finds compensating powers in other ways.

The strangest of all the renunciations is the eccentric but significant one of the provincial solicitor, Martineau, in *Strangers and Brothers* and *Time of Hope*. He withdraws from his firm, disburdens himself of all possessions, and becomes a wandering beggar-preacher. As worldly power and position go, it is only a very minor league that Martineau has left. Eliot is utterly unable to identify with this withdrawal. The incident is not of central importance to the scheme of the books. Yet Lewis is struck at every encounter with Martineau after the renunciation, by the man's appearance of serene happiness. He does not forget it. Snow shows us again and again that while power is inevitable and necessary, there is no peace for the individual exercising it. Yet, like the much misquoted biblical statement about money, it is not the fact of power but the immoderate love of it that is at the root of its evil.

In *The Masters*, the humane and decent Paul Jago hopes to be elected Master of his college. When the prize that seems within his grasp threatens to recede, he is appalled at what happens within him.

> Now it was in danger of being taken away: ashamed, beside himself, tormented, he was tempted to cheat, steal, and lie.

And this lust for power, this thirst for place, Lewis observes elsewhere, unlike the lust for women, does not abate with age.

The loss, or failure, of power—quite another matter from its renunciation—is seen in George Passant. The scale is small but the principle is universal. Though Passant is merely chief clerk in a small-town solicitor's office, he has a charismatic quality within his intimate circle. He is a generous friend and decisive factor in Lewis Eliot's life, for he helps him over the first hard hurdles of decision and action toward a career. Lewis, for his part, never forgets Passant. He stands by him in George's legal difficulties, and years later drags him, over official resistance, into the wartime civil service, and tries his best to secure his continuance in government work.

George's power is altogether rooted in an ability to cast over young people the personal spell of an articulate, enthusiastic, liberal, and slightly bohemian idealist. His power does not extend beyond the small circumference of his circle. The first cause of the loss of even this power is the public scandal and trial resulting from too closely shaved ethics in a business deal. The second is the simultaneous exposure of his decline within his group from inspirational leadership to sensual self-indulgence. The group would have disintegrated even if the trial had not occurred, because George, its cohesive force, had dissipated that force by his own self-deception.

The barrister, Herbert Getliffe, who pleads George's case, procures his acquittal. But in the process he describes the impairment of George's integrity and attributes it sententiously to the moral disorders of the times. Getliffe, who has risen to the silk (become a King's Counsellor), later falls short of his own ultimate ambition and power dream of a judge's robes because of a subtly tainted integrity that is a curious parallel to George's.

In his reflections, Lewis sums up Getliffe's closing speech at George's trial, as saying that in the future

> . . . the gentle, the friendly, the noble parts of us will survive alone. Yet at times he knew that it was not true. Sometimes he knew that the depths of harshness and suffering will go along with the gentle, corruptions and decadence along with the noble, as long as we are men.

George's failure haunts Lewis Eliot, who summarizes his friend as

> . . . the man who was larger than life, and yet capable of any self-deception; who was the most unselfseeking and generous of men, and yet sacri-

ficed everything for his own pleasures; who possessed formidable powers and yet was so far from
reality that they were never used; whose aims were
noble, and yet whose appetite for degradation was
as great as his appetite for life; who, in the depth of
his heart, was ill-at-ease, lonely, a diffident stranger
in the hostile world of men.

George is important to Snow—a little more, I con-
fess, than I can sustain, for I find him tedious at times,
and his story longer than is needed to make its point.
His return to the scene in *Homecomings* I did not
greet with enthusiasm. Yet Passant is a type of both
the stranger and the brother of the title of his own
book and the series. It is clear that Snow is emotionally involved in George's pattern of personality and
fascinated by this example of the failure of a considerable potential ever to realize itself as effective
power.

Perhaps the clearest statement about this bond is
Lewis's words in *Time of Hope:*

> I had known the depth of failure, and from that
> time I was bound to anyone who started with gifts
> and hope, and then felt his nature break him [Roy
> Calvert, too, and Charles March, and perhaps
> Martin Eliot and even Walter Luke the physicist
> in *The New Men,* in varying degrees]; I was bound
> not by compassion or detached sympathy, but be-
> cause I could have been his like, and might still be.

We are not to take too literally Lewis's expression of
his own failure—but it is the relative failure of an initial image of himself and his life, and the acceptance

of an adjusted pattern which is quite successful in its own terms.

A retrospective comment by Lewis in *The Affair* suggests another insight into his relations with George.

> As a young man, I had been fascinated by, and so had overvalued, the ambivalent, the tricky, the excessively fluid, and even now, though they no longer suggested to me the mystery of life as they once did, I had a weakness for them.

Roy Calvert, the young Cambridge orientalist, is one of Snow's most appealing and complex figures. The Manichees, whose ancient rite Roy studies as a scholar, provide the title for *The Light and the Dark,* and also the key to Roy's character. The Manichees saw the world as caught in a conflict between the power of light and the power of darkness, or good and evil, as coexistent and equal forces. Roy's temperament oscillates violently between a blithe, outgoing gaiety and joy of living, and a throttling melancholia in which some rash outburst is always latent. He is beautifully drawn in both his phases. His gaiety, his charm, which is persuasive to both men and women, his generosity and irrepressible humor are balanced against the secret, morbid withdrawal and despair, the death wish, and the hectic, rash public scenes that he creates in that mood. His central problem is an intense desire, confided to Lewis, for the religious belief which he is never able to accept.

When Snow's emotions are closely involved with an individual figure, he seems to protract the narrative to unnecessary length, to continue showing us something we have seen clearly, whereas in the more objective ensemble dramas he is almost unerring in his timing and proportion. I have protested this drawing-out about George Passant. It is somewhat true of Charles March, and even slightly so with Roy. His story begins to repeat its patterns and Lewis's mother-hen anxiety for Roy becomes tiresome.

Yet *The Light and the Dark* is a fine book, with many other excellent character studies and some of the most interesting observations of class patterns. Also it contains Snow's main study of the onset of World War II. The dark side of Roy is attracted for a time by the demonic Nazi movement as he has some contact with it in Germany. The war, when it comes, finds Roy unequivocally committed to England, but embracing combat as a covert means of pursuing his long-nurtured death wish. Roy is an important portrait of a complete individual, yet also represents the tragedy of a type, a class, and a generation in the England of the war.

When the preliminaries to the college election have begun in *The Masters*, it is Roy who utters the lines cited before:

> I want a man who knows something about himself. And is appalled. And has to forgive himself to get along.

This, I think, reflects one of Snow's deepest insights into character. It defines the only type of man we can trust. From as unlikely a source as the barrister Getliffe, at George Passant's trial, came words that bear on this:

> He wanted to build a better world . . . but it's fatal to build better worlds until you know what human beings are like and what you're like yourself. If you don't, you're liable to build, not a better world, but a worse one. . . .

Self-knowledge, then, is a major preoccupation in Snow's examination of character.

These insights are in harmony with the Judeo-Christian image of man in his creatureliness, so conspicuously lost in much modern fiction. The incapacity or refusal to be appalled at oneself, or the refusal or inability to forgive oneself, or the denial that forgiveness is necessary, are among the reasons why so many images of man become falsified or defective in contemporary writing.

In *The Masters* and *The Affair* his picture of political maneuvering in a microcosm is superb. The complexity, subtlety, and differentiation of types are remarkable. These men are a memorable group, to name only certain of them: Jago, Brown, Chrystal, Royce, Winslow, Nightingale, Crawford. Snow says of the Fellows, in *The Light and the Dark*, "They could stand more pomp than most bodies of men." The Master, Royce, remarks, "If you want to observe human nature in the raw . . . it's a very interesting point whether you ought to go out and find a pogrom or just watch some of our scientific colleagues competing for honors." These men are authentic in their special Cambridge world, and are only a part of the whole community there. Yet we are led to recognize their types, characters, and actions in projection into larger political frames. He sums up their natures again, within a different group, in *The New Men*, in terms that equally well apply to situations in almost all of the books:

> These men were fairer, and most of them a great deal abler, than the average: but you heard the same ripples below the words, as when any group of men chose anyone for any job. Put your ear to those meetings and you heard the intricate, labyrinthine and unassuageable rapacity, even in the best of men, of the love of power. If you have heard it once—say, in electing the chairman of a tiny dramatic society, it does not matter where—you have heard it in colleges, in bishoprics, in ministries, in cabinets: men do not alter because the issues they decide are bigger scale.

The Masters shows a mere thirteen men electing one of themselves to a largely honorific leadership. The struggle is fierce and subtle, and one of its most significant occurrences is that all agree on no account to permit deadlock to take the choice from their hands and delegate it to an outsider. The conservation of power is one of its principles.

A minor corollary of power is prerogative. We see

this jealously guarded also, in the functions of the Fellows of the college, even in the person of Snow's most affectionately comic characterization, the genially senile authority on the sagas, M. H. L. Gay.

In *The Affair* again we have a struggle within a small band of Fellows. The issue here is the rectifying of an alleged injustice. Snow has given stature to the case by making the victim both politically and personally objectionable to almost all the men involved in the decision. Doing objective justice in such a case is the same challenge as loving the unlovable.

In a brief prefatory note to *The Conscience of the Rich*, Snow discloses what is for him "the inner design" of the series.

> It consists of a resonance between what Lewis Eliot sees and what he feels. Some of the more important emotional themes he observes through others' experience, and then finds them enter into his own.

The latent temptation to cruelty which Lewis discerns in Charles March he feels in himself. Also Snow links the possessive love of Mr. March for his son in *The Conscience of the Rich* to Lewis's relations with his brother Martin in *The New Men* and to his struggle to establish a new marriage in *Homecomings*.

As a boy, Lewis had seen his mother's fierce ambition and had been fired by it. He sees it awake later in Martin. As the mother had nursed her own image of Lewis ("I expect big things from you, dear"), so has he done for Martin, and it is necessary for the younger brother to shake free.

The early emotional tensions between Lewis and his mother emerge as factors in his two marriages.

> Somehow I was so made that I had to reject my mother's love and all its successors. Some secret caution born of a kind of vanity made me bar my heart to any who forced their way within.

This leads to his unfortunate first marriage to Sheila, who offers him nothing and upon whom he must expend exhausting emotional effort. The old inability to accept an offered love, and to share a personal burden with his beloved; the wish to keep his "inner self inviolate," nearly destroy his later relationship with Margaret and drive her into another marriage before, at last, she and Lewis are united. That happy issue is possible only after Lewis has learned that he cannot possess her without sharing his whole self with her, and after both experience the profound purgation of having to owe the life of their child to the medical skill of Margaret's first husband.

We have seen that with the themes of power and renunciation there are links from book to book. The complete working out of the thematic inner structure of the series will not be visible until the completion of three more books; all present discussion, therefore, is predicated upon a still unfolding project. Even in the available volumes, the attempt to trace all the interwoven themes would require a detailed textual study not possible in a general essay.

Snow's insights into power and politics are carried onto their largest stage in *The New Men*, his fascinating story of science and government in wartime. It touches the problems of security, the myth of scientific secrets, and the moral dilemma of the scientists in relation to their handiwork in nuclear weapons. With this begins a shift of our present attention from Snow as novelist-craftsman to the social philosopher. *The New Men* is a natural link to the important themes that have spilled over from the novels and been concentrated in his published Rede and Godkin Lectures, *The Two Cultures and the Scientific Revolution*, and *Science and Government*.

Cultures or Communities?

I have a quarrel with the implications of the title, *The New Men*. Here, as in another instance to follow, Snow has been unfortunate in his choice of terms, the more so because these terms are highly effective. They contribute to a pattern of popular thought, a popular image, which is a barrier to the clarity of understanding which he insists must be attained in our world of the scientific revolution.

It would have been well if Snow had resisted the temptation to call his nuclear scientists "new men." It is the excellent achievement of the book to show us precisely that they are *not* new men but, alas, very much the old ones, whether you want to consider them as subject to the id or to original sin. The basic thing that is *not* new in the nuclear age is the human nature of its scientific brain trust. Their best is no better, their worst no worse, their average not conspicuously higher or lower, in terms of character, than the generality of their peers in other fields. Their capacity for agreement on principle or policy is not intrinsically greater than others'. Snow permits himself to say, in *The Two Cultures*, that scientists are perhaps the most moral, or morally concerned, men of the day. I challenge that, believing them to represent essentially the same character spectrum and capacity for judgment as other responsible and educated men.

When he adds that "almost all scientists form their own judgments of the moral life," I am not enthused. I have read too many of those judgments in my generation. Snow has remarked, concerning scientists' revulsion at much that they read in modern literature, "it is ill-considered of scientists to judge writers on the evidence of the period 1914–50." About scientists as moral sages, when I ponder some of the mischievous private moral nonsense a few individuals have brought forward as if somehow under the aura of science, I reverse Snow's admonition and make myself remember that it is ill-considered of writers to judge scientists by some spokesmen of the period 1914–61.

The whole texture of *The New Men* demonstrates my point, as does *Science and Government*. This is why I regret that the title of the novel contributes at all to the unhelpful and even dangerous popular myth of a new species of men, with overtones of supermen, which it is not Snow's intention to promulgate.

The other unsatisfactory expression, which is used to make a valid and important point, is "the two cultures." The phrase has captured attention and served to open an urgent discussion, but it is not adequately or accurately enough descriptive of the break in communication to be serviceable in the continued dialogue that should follow. Snow admits problems in the phrase and explains:

> I was searching for something a little more than a dashing metaphor, a good deal less than a cultural map: and for those purposes the two cultures is about right, and subtilizing any more would bring more disadvantages than it's worth.

Fair enough, for his original statement, which was both valuable and eloquent. It would not be worth disputing a phrase for a mere quibble. But I think it needs to be done in clarification and in response to the challenge in the situation that Snow has described for us.

In effect, he says that scientists and literary people have ceased to communicate with each other. They no longer understand one another. The writer does not know the technical language in which the scientist's experience of the world is couched; the scientist sometimes has contempt for the vision of life he sees reflected in some contemporary literature. Undoubtedly this is a serious schism at a crucial time in the race's history. But clarification of terms might be of some help in seeking a remedy.

Science is not a culture. It is one of the most brilliant, and as Snow justly says, most beautiful products or achievements of the culture in which it has developed for centuries, with an extraordinary, even appalling, acceleration in the present one. It now promises (or threatens—take your choice) to be the dominant aspect of the culture in the immediate future. That is the scientific revolution. It is this acceleration that has led to the schism with other parts of the culture.

This culture, so affected by the scientific revolution, is the only culture in man's history which could have bred modern science. Buddhist and Hindu attitudes toward the material universe were complete blocks to natural science. Modern science, now so avidly embraced in the East, exists there in a curious incongruity with surviving religious-philosophical concepts that prevented its indigenous growth. It was the great Judeo-Christian-Hellenic synthesis that prepared the seedground of Western science. It was the culture of Western Christendom that brought it to flower. That fruition is a communal achievement at the end of centuries of communal achievements. As Snow puts it, science "is moving in time."

Literature, even in its broadest definition, is not a culture either, but is the articulate voice of an important and variegated segment of it. Literature is not a science, but science often is a contributor to literature. The great scientific documents and definitions have always passed into the cultural heritage which literature embodies.

Culture, then, is a confusing and inaccurate word for either side of the division Snow discusses. There are various alternatives. To me, much the best is "community." There are numerous discrete, yet overlapping, communities within any culture. There is the intellectual community as a whole, of which the scientific community is a major wing. Snow reports the distinguished Cambridge mathematician, G. H. Hardy, saying to him, in the 1930's: "Have you noticed how the word 'intellectual' is used nowadays? There seems to be a new definition which certainly doesn't include Rutherford or Eddington or Dirac or Adrian or me. It does seem rather odd, don't y'know."

Actually, then, Snow is describing a growing schism in what Jacques Barzun calls the House of Intellect. The danger is that the house divided against itself cannot stand. A single major split would be bad enough, but there is great danger of further fragmentation. If scientists and literary people are communicating insufficiently with each other, then both communities are even more drastically cut off from communication with a vast mass population which is non-scientific and largely non-reading. This fact is potentially catastrophic in democratic societies where government policies are swayed by popular opinion.

Edward Teller is much exercised over this problem. He notes that people at large, and also many in political leadership, are uninformed on such emotionally loaded problems as fallout. Whether about this subject, or others related to science and survival, Teller worries because "a firm popular opinion can be formed on a completely erroneous basis. This popular opinion has a powerful influence on the government of our country." *

The immediate and vital problem in our education is to close the gaps that have opened between branches of the intellectual community, and then to work for a better contact between all parts of it and the non-reading public at large.

J. Robert Oppenheimer is only one of those who have pointed out that, amid the rapid breakthroughs in contemporary science, men in physics are hard put to keep abreast of the various segments of their own field, let alone the fields of others. At the same time, the profound unity subsuming physics, chemistry, and biology grows ever clearer. The need for advanced mathematics as the medium of expression and exchange of thought becomes greater in all of them, whereas it was once believed that the biologist did not need the mathematical equipment of the others.

Manifestly, the restored communication between the wings of the intellectual community, let alone

* "Education in an Age of Accelerated Science," in *Schools and Scholarship; The Christian Idea of Education, Part II.* Edited by Edmund Fuller. Yale University Press. 1962.

that between it and a larger public, cannot be achieved through technical training or advanced study on the part of non-scientists. The necessary dialogue is possible without the obviously impossible mutual mastery of fields. Spokesmen are the key—some from each side, and some who, like Snow, unusual in this respect but not unique, have a foot in each community.

Snow speaks of the complacency in literary circles, a tendency to regard scientists as "ignorant specialists" badly read in English literature. He has thrown out the counter-challenge of asking literary people to describe the Second Law of Thermodynamics, "the scientific equivalent of: *Have you read a work of Shakespeare's?*" Or asking what is meant in physics by mass or acceleration, "which is the scientific equivalent of saying, *Can you read?*" These are fair questions, which even a reasonable reading of popularized science, or a biography of Newton, should equip anyone to answer. Snow balances the complaint impartially, showing that the self-impoverishment is mutual, citing a distressing lack of acquaintance on the part of scientists with standard items of literary background. He admits ruefully the existence of some scientists to whom Dickens is a "type-specimen of literary incomprehensibility."

It is curious that although Snow knows the circles of literature, theatre, and art, he has not projected them in any of the novels, except most obliquely and briefly in *Homecomings*. We can hope he will draw upon some of these in one of the novels that will complete the series.

There must be a will if we are to restore the broken dialogue between the communities. Such a will can be aroused in proper education. Spokesmen are already there, but still more are needed. The literary and political communities cannot plead unavailability of means to understand the basic nature, purposes and processes of the scientific community. Many distinguished scientists have written admirably for the layman. There are also skilled journalists who have made themselves effective interpreters.

As for what it means to be a scientist, and the intellectual and emotional experiences of scientific life, we have had some glimpses in fiction and are bound to have more. Snow himself offers them to us in *The Search* and *The New Men* (the former is the only one of his novels not in the Lewis Eliot series).

Also, the best of what is called science fiction, sometimes written by scientists themselves, can make a real contribution to general understanding of the implications of the scientific age, by means of imaginative, often intuitively prophetic extrapolations from a present base of knowledge. Those literary intellectuals who scorn the genre and will not trouble to discriminate between the good and the bad are not wise in their generation. A non-scientist well read in high-level science fiction was better equipped than any other layman to read intelligently his morning paper on August 6, 1945, when the news of the bomb burst upon the public.

We had better give a moment's attention to scientific popularization, for it has a responsible role to play. To some it is anathema, and they are wrong who hold it so. If the term has become hopelessly pejorative a new one should be found. A book is best read in its original language. Science is completely understood only from within its disciplines. Yet it is better to know a great work in translation than not to know it at all. It is better for a layman to read about science in popularizations than to be starkly ignorant of it. But we want the best translations and we must have sound popularizations.

There are ways of closing the gap at several levels. The key factor is attitude. Nothing can be done if no one gives a damn about what lies beyond his own pasture. Snow's great service is the attempt to motivate a new attitude. A bridge is useless unless it is crossed voluntarily from both sides. It is an obligation upon the scientific community to keep the rest of us informed by a high standard of popularization, and by broadly conceived courses for non-scientists in schools and colleges. A notable example of this is a course of lectures in general science offered by Edward Teller at Berkeley. He has described it and given its basic reading list in the address previously quoted. The lectures themselves will be published in due course. This is a striking attempt at a rapproche-

ment on the part of an eminent physicist who found
it worth his time and energy to teach those who were
not entering his field. It is one of the chief ways of
drawing the communities closer.

The main front of the problem is in the education
of new generations, more than in the influencing of
present ones, many of whose attitudes are set. Secondary education is apt to be more crucial than the
college and university, to the extent that there the
intellectual awakening often occurs, there the commitment of interest begins. There the manifest non-
scientist should already learn that awareness of science is essential; there the awakening scientist should
find his needed roots in the other communities of
his culture.

Another schism—an artificial one—sometimes exists
between members of the scientific community and
those of the religious community. It is partly a result
of the myth of inherent conflict between these areas
of experience generated by celebrated clashes in past
history, and much-publicized opinions of relatively
few individuals on either side. Snow remarks that he
has known scientists with faith in revealed religion
and speculates that perhaps for them the sense of the
tragic condition is not so strongly felt as by other
scientists.

This subject is large and not to be pursued here,
yet it does touch the question of rifts in the intellectual community, and that of the grounds for moral
philosophy. A remarkable discussion of the whole

topic, to which I owe my choice of the term community as a counter-suggestion to Snow's cultures, is to be found in *Physicist and Christian: A Dialogue Between the Communities*, by William Grosvenor Pollard (Seabury Press, 1961).

To turn finally to the great problem of science and government, which Snow has discussed so interestingly, those two communities never again will be so far apart as they were before Einstein sent his famous wartime letter on nuclear fission to President Roosevelt. But this leads us back again to the fact that scientists are not new men. The impact of Snow's *Science and Government* lies in its demonstration of how dangerous it might be to have the wrong man get access to the right ear. There have been challenges of Snow's account of F. A. Lindemann's famous feud with Henry Tizard about radar and strategic bombing, in the high circles of England's wartime government. (The debate on bombing policy is reflected briefly in the latter parts of *The Light and the Dark* and in *The New Men* as well.) Whatever the merits of that case, the ultimate lesson of the lectures is that science is not a monolithic wisdom. "Various kinds of fear distort scientific judgments, just as they do other judgments," Snow says. So do pride and every force at work in the unconscious. When the scientist advises the statesman, both remain fallible and opinionated human beings, even when, at the best, they may be genuinely great ones.

On the socio-economic and political aspects of the scientific revolution, Snow is concerned both as an Englishman and a world citizen. As an Englishman, he knows that his country, no longer the seat of Empire, is therefore no longer self-sufficient economically or militarily. He observes that, "The only real assets we have, in fact, are our wits." In her economic relations with the world, England must use her energy and ingenuity, her scientific and engineering creativity, to hold herself in productive competition. But this is not just an English problem. So long as the cold war stays cold, the challenge to the West is to show that modern science and industry can meet the needs of the underdeveloped countries under a free form of society.

> Once the trick of getting rich is known, as it now is, the world can't survive half rich and half poor . . . The West has got to help in this transformation. The trouble is, the West with its divided culture finds it hard to grasp just how big, and above all just how fast, the transformation must be.

Snow is the best present moderator between the scientific and literary communities. His importance in literature rests not only on his considerable skill and substance as a novelist, but also on the scope of his vision and his responsible concern with the great issues of his time in science, government, and education. He has said that if we yield to the idea that things have gotten too big for us, we are lost. ". . . we've got to act as though they're not," Walter Luke says, in *The New Men.* The best guard against such a feeling of being overwhelmed by events is foresight, "which our kind of existential society is desperately short of." Snow believes that scientists can contribute foresights of a unique order. That is true, but theirs is not the only foresight needed. There are equal need and obligation for the artist to contribute his intuitive foresights about our developing future. Unless the artist can do this with sanity, courage, faith and wisdom, grounded in a comprehension of our human nature, our Western heritage, and the challenges and realities of the scientific revolution, he will have failed us. This is C. P. Snow's challenge to both communities.

It is the opposite of Snow's qualities—solipsistic and self-pitying isolation, craven retreats from responsibility, and denials that life has meaning—that have put one large wing of the literary community out of touch with the constructive stream of our age, and even with many of their fellow artists. Where some writers have withdrawn in complaint, to mutter among themselves, Snow represents the vigorous, honorable tradition of the literary man who applies his mind and talents to the effort to understand and interpret his time, to shape the immediate future of his world, and to meet the challenge with which that world confronts us.

A note on the fantastic

He who does not imagine in stronger and better lineaments and in stronger and better light than his perishing and mortal eye can see, does not imagine at all.
—*William Blake*

By the forging of Gram cold iron was revealed; by the making of Pegasus horses were ennobled; in the Trees of the Sun and Moon root and stock, flower and fruit are manifested in glory.
—*J. R. R. Tolkien*

From the primitive folk origins of myth and fairy tale to the most sophisticated conscious literary art, the fantastic story has been beloved of men. It is as old as literature and will remain as long as any form of the storyteller's skill is practiced.

It must be understood that there are several kinds of private fantasy, from the dangerously pathological delusion to the harmless daydream. What concerns us here is none of these, but solely the consciously projected, controlled literary fantasy. Even it has many genres and sub-classifications, including fairy tales, fables, animal tales, ghost stories, Utopias, and science fiction. Fantasy has high entertainment value and has been much practiced for that legitimate end alone. Yet across the range of time and type of story, the so-called fantastic has also served to illuminate our understanding of the so-called real.

Good fantasy is not escapist in the pejorative sense of that word. Indeed it may offer temporary refuge and relief from the pressure of an immediate world. But if it is of depth, we are brought to a deeper pondering and insight into central aspects of our actual lives. Our sensitivity is whetted to honor and courage and aspiration and beauty. No one thinking on these things is escaping reality; to cling to them in our daily world is a hard, often nearly impossible, challenge and struggle. Yet without them high in our consciousness, life is immeasurably debased. The integrity and courage of an imaginary being in his world may sustain us to integrity and courage in the face of a mundane and pressing dilemma in our own living.

The literary notion of realism, the idea that reality can be represented accurately and fully in art, is a relatively late flower. What it really means is the close portrayal of observed behavior, setting, and event, with the implication about its segment of life, "This is how it really is." Realism in this special sense enjoyed a tremendous, at times nearly monopolistic, vogue between the mid-nineteenth and mid-twentieth centuries. It has an honorable and permanent place and function in literature. We could not do without it as one of the modes in which the writer approaches life—whereas some of the earliest enthusiasts of realism thought we could thereafter get along without fantasy.

For the satirist, the moralist, the philosopher, the theologian, or any other ponderer of the human condition who might reject any of those labels, the fantastic tale offers an approach to reality that literal slices of life are unable to match. This is why Thornton Wilder, who has worked with fantastic freedom in such a play as *The Skin of Our Teeth*, speaks of trying "to capture not verisimilitude but reality." So much of existence, its meanings and its values, the nature of Creation, the counterpoise between good and evil, the relation between man and God, remains a mystery that the approach to many areas of experience is possible only through imaginative images and symbols.

Fantasy is an art of equivalents. It says, "Reality is like this—but not literally this." Its mysteries, intangibles and enigmas involve the profoundest questions of man. That is why when the great fantasist has stepped outside the bounds of what we conventionally call reality (for of course that is no such thing, but only a tiny observed segment of the whole spectrum of being) we are suddenly conscious that he has revealed truths about ourselves. We see this sharply exemplified in a rare context when so great a master of the realistic as Dostoyevsky steps from that mode in the midst of *The Brothers Karamazov*, to write "The Grand Inquisitor," that majestic, fantastic heart of one of all literature's most powerfully realistic books.

The peculiar kind of reality of its own which the imaginative work of art takes on may become more vital, living and persistent than any supposed actuality of history. We have no identifiable historical counterpart for Homer's Achilles (or for Homer), yet Homer is a powerful reality and so is Achilles. What men of flesh and blood died on the grounds of the place that was Troy we shall never know. They vanished into the soil; they do not exist for us.

But the fictitious Achilles speaks of the alternative paths of his destiny as his goddess mother has revealed them to him (exemplifying an element of choice present even in the Greek concept of fate):

> If I stay here and play my part in the siege of Troy, there is no home-coming for me, though I shall win undying fame. But if I go home to my own country my good name will be lost, though I shall have long life, and shall be spared an early death. (*Iliad*, E. V. Rieu's translation)

And so he stayed, and died, and so far as human terms are concerned, his name and fame are undying. It would take the total destruction of our literary and proverbial culture—indeed even of the vocabulary of anatomy—to wipe the name of Achilles from the memory of man. Which then is more real—the nameless flesh and blood absorbed centuries ago in Anatolian soil, or the indestructible, living fiction, Achilles?

Among the rewards of fantasy are what J. R. R. Tolkien calls "the satisfaction of certain primordial human desires." He cites as examples of these the desire "to survey the depths of space and time," and "to hold communion with other living things," such as animals and birds, trees, fairies, dwarfs, or angels.

Much that is familiar and matter-of-fact—what we think of as *real*—is present in fantasy, augmented by the dimension of the fantastic. That dimension, as often in the novels of Charles Williams, may be represented solely through one fact, or event, or presence, within the pattern of the recognizable. (It is so in T. S. Eliot's *The Cocktail Party*.) Or else it may be the whole of another world, richly exotic and strangely peopled—yet there are points of reference always to tie it to ourselves.

The response to fantasy requires the preservation of the sense of wonder, a ready acceptance, and a self-giving. Some people cannot or will not enter its world. Extreme cases of this sort often have sought to forbid fantasy to children, holding it to be either frivolous or baleful. If you bring nothing into the world of wonder you will go away from it unfilled.

There are three contemporary masters of the fantastic story whom I wish to discuss: C. S. Lewis,

J. R. R. Tolkien, and Charles Williams. They belong naturally in a related study. Each is English, each has a Christian view of the nature of reality. They were friends whose association, especially during the years of World War II, cross-fertilized one another's works. The three-way exchange was broken by Williams's death in 1945. C. S. Lewis is the most widely known and read, both in the United States and England. Williams and Tolkien also have an American as well as English following which is growing steadily.

No man can write richly textured fantasy as if it had never been written before. There is a cumulative heritage on which all must build to some extent. Thus real or apparent sources and influences always can be found. A specific inspiration and influence upon these three—but most notably, by his own acknowledgment, upon Lewis—is the Victorian writer, George MacDonald. He has been known to generations of children through *The Princess and the Goblin*, *The Princess and Curdie*, and *At the Back of the North Wind*.

All devotees of fantasy should know his adult books, *Phantastes* and *Lilith*, written respectively at the beginning and the end of his career. They are available together in an American reprint under the title *The Visionary Novels of George MacDonald*, Edited by Anne Fremantle with a Preface by W. H. Auden (Noonday Press, 1954). Unfortunately *Phantastes* has been marred both in effect and meaning by the omission of poems in the text, and chapter-head mottoes of great significance. Still, this is the only version in print of an important work.

For further knowledge of MacDonald and sources of influence upon him, see Robert Lee Wolff's *The Golden Key: A Study of the Fiction of George MacDonald* (Yale University Press, 1961). It is an excellent study, though weighted too heavily toward Freudian interpretation of MacDonald's motivations as writer.

The discussions that follow are undertaken in the dual hope of contributing to the further appreciation of Lewis, Tolkien, and Williams by those who have made their acquaintance already, and even more important, of introducing them to new circles of readers.

I have spoken of them together as novelists and have been reproached on occasion for doing so. Their merit is not affected by however they are classified. I will cheerfully settle for them all as story-tellers. Yet they cannot so lightly be excluded from that vast and varied canon that is the novel. It knows few boundaries of form and style; it is not to be limited to the realistic mode or to the conventional matter of any period. A fantastic frame of time and space is no disqualifier. The novels of C. S. Lewis are true novels, though three of them can be classified as science fiction and the fourth is a retelling of a myth. The novels of Charles Williams cannot be thrust into any ready pigeonhole. Generally they begin in a frame of the most deceptively everyday realism, but suddenly Williams begins to open doors and windows from what we commonly call the natural to the supernatural. He moves us into further dimensions of what many of us accept as reality, not literally but, again, by image and symbol. These strange dimensions do not alter the nature of the books as novels.

Tolkien is the most special case of the three. His big work can be called a romance, a saga, an epic, or a fairy tale. If you wish, just call it a story. Any of these, or other, labels may be useful. Yet, as a long prose fiction, introducing and developing an enormous cast of characters and carrying them through a complete and carefully plotted pattern of meaningful experience, I do not see how one can refuse it recognition as a novel, atypical, indeed unique, though it is.

Hence, I call these men novelists. They are conspicuous among their contemporaries for using different modes from the major fashions of the period. They are also conspicuous for offering exceptionally powerful images of man, his nature, his destiny, his choices, and the environment which contains him. It is for these considerations, apart from others, that I rank them high, and assert their importance among the storytellers of our time.

The Christian spaceman: C. S. Lewis

A space ship from Earth has landed on Mars. The hatch opens and three men tumble out. Two of them have been there before, but for Ransom—and for us —it is all new:

> The air was cold but not bitterly so, and it seemed a little rough at the back of his throat. He gazed about him, and the very intensity of his desire to take in the new world at a glance defeated itself. He saw nothing but colors—colors that refused to form themselves into things. Moreover, he knew nothing yet well enough to see it: you cannot see things till you know roughly what they are. His first impression was of a bright, pale world—a water-color world out of a child's paint-box; a moment later he recognized the flat belt of light blue as a sheet of water, or of something like water, which came nearly to his feet. They were on the shore of a lake or river.

Ransom is a most unlikely space traveler: a round-shouldered, unathletic philologist from Cambridge.

And indeed he is on Mars only because he has been kidnapped by the other two men. Not long afterwards he escapes from them and in his flight encounters a being of an unknown kind, rather like a seven-foot otter. Ransom's dread is to some extent conquered by his curiosity as a philologist when he hears it making sounds that are unmistakably language, but it is a terrifying moment. Nevertheless, it is "the first tingling intercourse of two different, but rational, species," and not until much later does he have a chance to reflect on his misgivings.

> It was only many days later that Ransom discovered how to deal with these sudden losses of confidence. They arose when the rationality of the *hross* tempted you to think of it as a man. Then it became abominable—a man seven feet high, with a snaky body, covered, face and all, with thick black animal hair, and whiskered like a cat. But starting from the other end you had an animal with everything an animal ought to have—glossy coat, liquid eye, sweet breath, and whitest teeth—and added to all these, as though Paradise had never been lost and earliest dreams were true, the charm of speech and reason. Nothing could be more disgusting than the one impression; nothing more delightful than the other. It all depended on the point of view.

What have we here? Space opera à la Buck Rogers or Flash Gordon? No—not with this style and such subtleties of perception as the fact that we cannot really "see" what we do not know, and the two ways of looking at another species. High-quality science fiction, then? Not quite that either. This story forms a category of its own, even though it *is* good science fiction.

The best clue is in the phrase "as though Paradise had never been lost." For indeed this Mars ("Malacandra" to its own people) is an unfallen world. It is described in a book called *Out of the Silent Planet*, the first novel of a trilogy that is continued in *Perelandra* and *That Hideous Strength*. All three are adventure stories in the mode of science fiction. But under the trappings lies something else: Christian theology projected beyond Earth and man, a theology of the universe in the dawn of the space age. This is the work of an extraordinary Englishman, master of a number of intellectual and artistic trades: C. S. Lewis.

Clive Staples Lewis holds a chair in Medieval and Renaissance English Literature at Cambridge University. The two most specialized of his books are the fruits of his scholarly labors: the fat volume on the sixteenth century in the *Oxford History of English Literature* and *The Allegory of Love*, a medieval study. His other books range from a partial autobiography through a variety of fiction and nonfiction, including a wonderful series for children.

The mainspring of all these writings is the fact that Lewis is a believing Christian (Anglican in affiliation), and his primary fame is as the most imaginative and versatile of Christian apologists.

A few of his books are traditional apologetics,

straightforwardly didactic. *Mere Christianity* (developed from a notable series of BBC talks), *Miracles*, and *The Problem of Pain* are good examples and are enough to distinguish him in this field. But for all their merit such books of argumentation would not have built his following and his reputation. His finest apologetics are in the series of fantastic novels which disclose as rich a gift for sheer imaginative writing as our all-too-literal age can boast. Once again the artist and the spinner of tales proves the best persuader.

Lewis was converted to Christianity from atheism. In the nature of such matters, the preparatory processes were prolonged, the moment of actual crossover from the sense of no-God to the sense of God was abrupt, and the subsequent progression from general theism to specific theology was again a more gradual evolution. He has given us his own account of this history in *Surprised by Joy*. But a sensitive reader will perceive that in the popular *Screwtape Letters* he has also objectively and obliquely described many separate stages of the conversion experience.

He was born in 1898 in Ireland, some touch of which land may have contributed to his gifts as a fantasist. From a home that was nominally religious (Protestant), he went through the mills of education (graphically reported in a vein that has much in common with Orwell's "Such, Such Were the

Joys") and emerged an "enlightened" atheist. At nineteen he stumbled upon the book *Phantastes* by the Victorian mystic and novelist George MacDonald. Of that experience he testifies:

> My imagination was, in a certain sense, baptized; the rest of me, not unnaturally, took longer. I had not the faintest notion what I had let myself in for by buying *Phantastes*. I met there all that had already charmed me in Malory, Spenser, Morris, and Yeats. But in another sense all was changed. I did not yet know (and I was long in learning) the name of the new quality, the bright shadow, that rested on the travels of Anodos. I do now. It was Holiness.

The conversion seeded by MacDonald, and watered later by G. K. Chesterton and a variety of personal relationships, flowered at Oxford when Lewis was thirty-one: "That which I greatly feared had at last come upon me. In the Trinity Term of 1929 I gave in, and admitted that God was God, and knelt and prayed; perhaps, that night, the most dejected and reluctant convert in all England."

Except for service in World War I, in which he was wounded (he first read Chesterton in an army hospital), Lewis has led a wholly academic life, sharing his home with his older brother, W. H. Lewis, also a writer, especially on seventeenth-century France. A few years ago he married an American, Joy Davidman, herself a talented poet and novelist, and also a convert (in part through the influence of Lewis's writings, long before meeting him). She died in 1960.

C. S. Lewis shows us reality through fantasy and symbol, which, as the mythmakers and poets always have known, are the closest approaches to elusive reality that we can make. The reality structure he offers us is that proclaimed by Christianity. To the Christian it is truth, to the non-Christian, a tale.

Modern fiction is dominated by so-called realism, which glories in its imitation of the technique of reporting. The claim to realness lies in the fact that many things (including an unstinting catalogue of revolting things) which people in fiction are portrayed as doing are indeed done by people in life. In itself, this coincidence does not in any way assure the over-all reality.

Attempts to portray the reality of life (which can be only approximate at best) succeed to the degree to which they manage to capture and reflect glimpses of the total reality of who we are, what we are, and where we are. The error of confining literature to "realism" is the supposition that what we see, hear, feel, taste, smell, or think can be dignified by so presumptuous a word as "real." At the most it is a fragment of reality, as the mystic and the physicist alike can testify.

In one of Lewis's books for children there is a conversation about a star. "In our world," a boy says, "a star is a huge ball of flaming gas." He is answered:

"Even in your world, my son, that is not what a star is but only what it is made of." In the same spirit, we cannot equate a human being with the wretched few pennies' worth of chemical elements of which our bodies are composed. Our reality is more than what we are made of.

Possibly the most famous of Lewis's single works is the little volume called *The Screwtape Letters*. With wit and grace it ranges over a wide swath of Christian thought by the device of seeing it from the enemy camp. It is a series of letters from a minor administrative devil, Screwtape, to his nephew, a junior tempter named Wormwood, advising him on the campaign for the soul of the human being to whom Wormwood has been assigned. The inexperienced tempter is counseled not to let his subject acquire

> the fatal habit of attending to universal issues and withdrawing his attention from the stream of immediate sense experiences. Your business is to fix his attention on the stream. Teach him to call it "real life" and don't let him ask what he means by "real" . . . Keep pressing home on him the *ordinariness* of things.

Man urgently needs for his intellectual and spiritual health the recovery and preservation of wonder, awe, radical amazement, the sense of the Holy. We require the breaking down of what Lewis calls "our nature's incurable incredulity," for it is the vulgar error of our day to believe too little rather than too much. The real fool is he who is so afraid of being gulled that he will not permit himself belief. The true gulls of history are not those few who have purchased Brooklyn Bridge, or gold bricks, or phony mining shares, they are those who have stood by at every great invention and discovery, and croaked, "It won't work," "It'll never get off the ground," "There's nothing across the ocean," "I won't look through the telescope because there's nothing to see," or "Don't ask me to believe that little invisible animals make people sick." Accordingly, many of us have

> eased the burden of intolerable strangeness which this universe imposes on us by dividing it into two halves (natural and supernatural) and encouraging the mind never to think of both in the same context.

The "realist" invokes the "laws of Nature" against the "miraculous." But

> the Laws of the universe are never broken. Your mistake is to think that the little regularities we have observed on one planet for a few hundred years are the real unbreakable laws.

Chad Walsh, in the only book-length study of Lewis and his work to date (though there is now a large body of important work not included in it), called him "Apostle to the Skeptics." With equal aptness, he is Apostle to the Space Age. He uses the resources of contemporary imagination, blended freely with motifs from classical mythology, as vehicles for eternal inquiries. Lewis sees in mythology "the childhood of religion . . . a prophetic dream"; Christianity fulfills "the hints of all Paganism. . . ." Thus his wonderful perception of why, inevitably, in a fallen world, "mythology was what it was—gleams of celestial strength and beauty falling on a jungle of filth and imbecility."

In his approach to fantasy as a storyteller, he is at pains to acknowledge—indeed to emphasize—that he regards George MacDonald as his master. He adopts a number of MacDonald's devices, especially in the children's books, in some of his choices of portals for passing from our dimension to that of the land he calls Narnia. In *The Great Divorce*, his contra-Blakeian fantasy on Heaven and Hell and how the soul must decide between them, he introduces the shade of MacDonald himself, as a sage in Purgatory, to give the narrator (Lewis, by implication) counsel about his dream.

To see Lewis's methods in operation, one should examine the trilogy that begins with *Out of the Silent Planet*. Taken at no other level than pure, enthralling adventure these are first-class stories, exuberantly inventive and especially notable for the descriptive evocation of strange worlds. Marjorie Hope Nicolson, in *Voyages to the Moon*, her excellent tracing of the long tradition of space-travel fantasy from ancient times, pays warm tribute to the visual richness and lyrical freshness of Lewis's description of Malacandrian scenes. These put him, she feels, in the first rank of the genre: *"Out of the Silent Planet . . .* is to me the most beautiful of all cosmic voyages and in some ways the most moving."

This ability to make imagined places visually intense in rich detail, which we find in all his stories, is an enviable natural endowment. He may have sharpened it by, or it may spring from the same source as, his appreciation of the gift in other writers. In an essay, "On Stories," in *Essays Presented to Charles Williams* (Oxford, 1947), he complains about a flaw in *The Three Musketeers.*

> The total lack of atmosphere repels me. There is no country in the book—save as a storehouse of inns and ambushes. There is no weather.

The deep roots of Lewis's scene-painting gifts are seen in a remark he makes in *An Experiment in Criticism* (1961), where he has many striking things to say about myth, fantasy, and story in general.

> I am probably one of many [that, I doubt] who, on a wakeful night, entertain themselves with invented landscapes. I trace great rivers from where the gulls scream at the estuary, through the windings of ever narrower and more precipitous gorges, up to the barely audible tinkling of their source in a fold of the moors.

It is certainly such intense and absorbed visualizing that has filled out the delights of Malacandrian, Perelandrian, and Narnian landscape for us.

The universe of Lewis is not the chilling wilderness of "space." To his hero, Ransom, bathed in the fearful glory between the worlds,

> the very name "Space" seemed a blasphemous libel . . . He could not call it "dead" . . . Since out of this ocean the worlds and all their life had come. He had thought it barren: he saw now that it was the womb of worlds . . . No: Space was the wrong name. Older thinkers had been wiser when they named it simply the heavens.

The overwhelming distances of astronomy, which leave the human helpless in the presence of immensity, Lewis wraps in the term "deep heaven." His universe is not lifeless, hostile, empty, or impersonal. It is the whole created realm of God, harmonious in the Great Dance, which is the motion of galaxies and stars and of all things, great and small, atom and organism. Some places in this universe are inhabited by beings analogous to man (as astronomy also believes), but elsewhere and everywhere by beings of other and higher orders—that complex hierarchy known alike to Christian, Jew, and Moslem as angels. Not to believe in this hierarchy is to presume a one-jump gap in powers and natures between man and God. Earth is one of the "low worlds." The great planets, Jupiter and Saturn, are the province of mighty, intelligent beings who are not organisms.

But at the opening of the trilogy Ransom does not know all this. On a hiking tour he blunders into the hands of a sinister pair named Weston and Devine, and the great adventure begins. Professor

Weston is a physicist of genius who has built a space ship. He represents the man-centered materialist to whom religion is superstition; his goal is no less than the colonization of the universe by man and the perpetuation of genus Homo. Devine, his financial backer and partner, is interested only in a cash return and embodies ruthless greed. Together they have already made one successful trip to Malacandra (Mars) and are about to embark on another. But they need a specimen of man to give to the ruler of that planet, they think for human sacrifice, and Ransom fortuitously becomes their intended victim.

The title *Out of the Silent Planet* is a clue to the meaning. Ransom, to whom the strange planet is at first a scene of terror, eventually realizes that the true place of horror is the world from which he has come, which is known on Malacandra as Thulcandra, the "Silent Planet." It lies behind a cosmic "iron curtain."

In the harmonious Creation our planet stands, uniquely, as enemy-occupied territory. In Lewis's scheme a great angel of a certain high category, I would say an archangel (in the language of Malacandra "Oyarsa," *pl.* "Oyéresu"), has in his charge each of the planets with all its beings. But the Oyarsa of Earth (Satan) alienated himself from God by the corruption of his own will—in the sin of Pride—together with a host of angelic adherents; he and they stand exiled from deep heaven, confined within the orbit of our moon. He who was the shep-

herd of the planet has seduced his charges into rebellion and evil after his own kind, and his influence
has led to their fall.

Here then is a twentieth-century variant of *Paradise Lost*, a fresh telling of the Christian myth of the
fall of man. (To call it a myth does not mean that it
is not true, it means that it states a truth in a symbolic story.) It dramatizes and clarifies for our age
the Christian teaching about man's peculiar dilemma
in the order of Creation. The tragic fact of man's
condition is that he is other than he was intended to
be; the deep springs of his will have been subverted—
he cannot do consistently the good that he would
do, but does instead the evil that he would not do.
The Incarnation is seen as an action from without, a
beachhead for the reconquest of the planet and the
redemption of man. This action, in God's methods,
is not an intervention by force but an invitation to
free wills. Anyone may believe and accept the proffered redemption, but no one is compelled to accept
it or to believe.

In contrast to our planet Lewis evokes the richly
imagined, unfallen world of Malacandra, where several distinct orders of intelligent beings with souls
live in harmony and obedience to their Creator
("whose service is perfect freedom").

Ransom is brought into the presence of the Oyarsa, or ruling angel, of Malacandra. From him Ransom
learns the truth about the history and condition of
his own planet. The machinations of Weston and

Devine are frustrated and all are sent back to earth in the ship that had brought them, Ransom under special protection from the malice of his co-travelers.

In the next book Ransom, now voluntarily co-operating with the great angels in the service of God, is sent on a special mission to the planet Perelandra (Venus). Here is an analogue of the Garden of Eden story. Yet, as Lewis insists, it is different, for it is subsequent, and God does not do large things twice in the same way.

A new Eve is confronted with temptation. In this exotically beautiful world of rippling, floating islands on vast warm seas, the forbidden act is to stay overnight on the fixed lands before an appointed time has come.

There is a subtle tempter, embodied in the person of Professor Weston, who has come there as the voluntary servant of the corrupt Oyarsa of Earth but is later, as we shall see, wholly possessed by him. Weston is the medium, or host, by which he has been able to violate the previous quarantine on his scope of influence. The newness of this Garden story is that *two* voices from the world that had known the tragedy of what Milton called "man's first disobedience" intervene in the decision which the woman of Perelandra must make. In short, where there had been one intervention (the serpent's) in Eve's fall, there is now a counter-intervention to argue against the seduction.

In this story Lewis deepens our understanding of

the nature of man's fall. We are given a poet's vision of what man was intended to be. The tempting of the first woman of Perelandra entails an extraordinarily intricate, far-reaching debate at the deepest level of moral theology.

Perelandra intensifies and extends all the qualities of *Out of the Silent Planet*. Intellectually it is much more exacting. Imaginatively and descriptively it is a more soaring flight, reaching its grand climax in a partial vision of the Great Dance, a kind of *Te Deum*, a praise of all the works of the Lord. It affirms that "All is gift." To any responsive reader it gives a unique experience, a purgation through exaltation and awe rather than the familiar Aristotelian one through pity and terror. It is the apex of the trilogy. At the time of this writing, the English composer Donald Swann and his librettist David Marsh have completed the ambitious undertaking of making an opera of *Perelandra*.

The third novel, *That Hideous Strength*, is a buoyant satire on the overweening pretensions of technology and the social sciences. Lewis had already gibed at the latter in *The Screwtape Letters*, in which the elder devil counsels the junior tempter:

Above all, do not attempt to use science (I mean, the real sciences) as a defence against Christianity. They will positively encourage him to think about realities he can't touch and see. There have been sad cases among the modern physicists. If he must dabble in science, keep him on economics and sociology.

In *That Hideous Strength* the forces of evil operate behind the front of a vast sociological institute with much money and political power: the N.I.C.E. (National Institute of Co-ordinated Experiments). Aspects of the N.I.C.E. are highly funny, but the picture grows grim as it reveals the intention, meaning, and motivation behind the boast that "this time we're going to get science applied to social problems and backed by the whole force of the state":

> It does really look as if we now had the power to dig ourselves in as a species . . . to take control of our own destiny. If Science is really given a free hand; it can now take over the human race and re-condition it: make man a really efficient animal.

It pictures an attempt at the dehumanization of man fully as deadly as those imagined by Huxley and Orwell, with the added value that Lewis's vision of the actual nature of man which is being violated is much more profoundly grounded than that of the other two. The N.I.C.E. plan aims at "Man Immortal and Man Ubiquitous . . . Man on the throne of the universe."

This vision, of course, is madness. The dream of man as supreme in Creation, with the ruthless totalitarianism that accompanies it, is inspired by the corrupt Oyarsa of Earth and his cohorts of banished angels. These are not known in their true nature to the men of the N.I.C.E., who would consider angels, good or bad, to be vulgar superstition.

But against this dreadful threat of enslavement by a dehumanizing tyranny, a counterforce is poised of a kind imagined by neither Huxley nor Orwell in their famous novels of dark prophecy. The human protagonists guided by Ransom—an elder statesman here who is now identified as the "Pendragon," the successor to King Arthur (in a mystical, not a political sense)—invoke the strength of Logres, the ancient Christian realm in the heart of England. Arthur's great magician, Merlin, is awakened from the magic sleep into which, in Malory's *Morte d'Arthur*, he had been cast. The great Oyéresu of the first two books lend their powers, through the voluntary vehicle of Merlin, so that the mighty coup prepared by the forces of the corrupted Oyarsa of Earth is thwarted.

In this sweeping theological fantasy, man is both reduced and exalted: reduced in the naked depiction of his self-wrought condition, exalted through the mystery of the Incarnation—that God became man for his salvation. In the trilogy, and also in an article called "Will We Lose God in Outer Space?" written for the *Christian Herald* in 1958, and subsequently included in a volume called *The Earth's Last Night and Other Essays*, Lewis examines the question of man's uniqueness. What of other beings possessing both intelligence and souls who may be elsewhere in the universe, if not in our solar system?

On some planets, somewhere, the equivalents of

man may be unfallen, still in the state God intended for them. If, elsewhere, there are other beings who have fallen, before or since man's fall, it is likely that God will have devised the appropriate means for their redemption, though not necessarily the same as the means for ours. That passionate skeptic, Mark Twain, far removed from Lewis's theology, had a similar idea in his story *Captain Stormfield's Visit to Heaven*. The Captain, entering Paradise by the wrong gate, is hard put to let the officials know from what obscure world he has come. (It turns out to be one contemptuously known as "the Wart.") "It's the one the Saviour saved," he says hopefully. The gateman bows his head at the Name, then says gently: "The worlds He has saved are like to the gates of heaven in number—none can count them."

John Donne, in one of his sermons, anticipated such a question by the alertness of his response to the new breakthroughs of astronomy in the Elizabethan and Jacobean age. He notes that "subtle men have, with some appearance of probability, imagined that in that heaven, in those manifold spheres of the planets and the stars, there are many earths, many worlds, as big as this which we inhabit. . . ." If it is so, he says, with an eye to the theological implications, we can be assured of "the merit and passion of Christ Jesus, sufficient to save millions of worlds. . . ."

Lewis, in his *Christian Herald* article, admonishes us against the interplanetary imperialism which Professor Weston attempts in *Out of the Silent Planet*.

Against the creatures we might find on other worlds, he fears that

> we shall, if we can, commit all the crimes we have already committed against creatures certainly human but differing from us in features and pigmentation . . . Our loyalty is due not to our species but to God. Those who are, or can become, His sons, are our real brothers, even if they have shells or tusks . . . It is spiritual not biological kinship that counts.

In the trilogy, Lewis focuses attention upon forms of the sin of pride: the desire to affirm man as God or as godlike, the ambition to dominate the universe, to supersede other species, to live forever.

He lays the basis for his thesis in an ingenious presentation of the doctrine of sin—an unpopular word in the modern vocabulary. The beings of his unfallen world, Malacandra, have no word for sin or evil. They grope for the concept through the word "bent." This is a most revealing monosyllable.

We never use "bent" to describe the *first state* of anything; hence it tells us that there was a previous condition. It contains various possibilities, though not certainties, of a future condition: restored to the original state, remaining the same, or becoming more bent to the point of being broken. When an object is bent it will be misshapen or will malfunction or will fail to function at all. A bent arrow or a bent gun will miss the mark. Christianity does not know evil as a separate entity, but understands all evil as the corruption of an original good, susceptible of a possible redemption. It is this corruption which is sin. Its home base is in the will.

In the trilogy, Weston, the space-conquering physicist, displays the most dangerous form of bentness. It is the corruption of great gifts and beyond the crude self-seeking of his partner, Devine. Weston would make man, and the seed of man, supreme. He declares to the Oyarsa of Malacandra:

> Life is greater than any system of morality; her claims are absolute . . . I am prepared without flinching to plant the flag of man on the soil of Malacandra: to march on, step by step, superseding, where necessary, the lower forms of life that we find, claiming planet after planet, system after system, till our posterity—whatever strange form and yet unguessed mentality they have assumed—dwell in the universe wherever the universe is habitable.

Of Weston's ambition, Oyarsa asks:

> Does he think he could go to the great worlds? Does he think Maleldil [God] wants a race to live forever?

Modern man ignores, and Lewis reminds him of, that portion of Christian doctrine called eschatology, or Last Things. It shocked many and made headlines several years ago when the Archbishop of Canterbury (then Dr. Fisher) said that God's purposes might contain the possibility of man destroying his species with the hydrogen bomb. But in Lewis's words, there is "now at last a real chance for fallen Man to shake off that limitation of his powers which mercy had imposed upon him as a protection from the full results of his fall."

In *Perelandra* Weston finally delivers himself wholly into the power of the lord of the silent planet, the "bent Oyarsa" (Satan), by the rash words, "I call that Force into me completely." As he is rent by the paroxysms of demonic possession, the true Weston dies while his body remains an "unman," a walking, speaking shell, animated by the Power with whom Ransom must wage his portentous struggle in direct and deadly combat. Lewis's specific point here is that demonic possession in any degree, like redemption, is not a matter of imposed outside force, but a matter of invitation. God will not force Himself upon the soul who does not invite Him, and Satan cannot.

I rate high among Lewis's accomplishments a work generally less well known, as yet, than the trilogy, but for which I predict a growing reputation and a long life. This is the series of seven books for children which composes the Chronicles of Narnia, published between 1950 and 1956. Not in order of their original appearance, but in the strict order of their internal chronology, they are: *The Magician's Nephew; The Lion, the Witch, and the Wardrobe; The Horse and His Boy; Prince Caspian; The Voy-*

age of the Dawn-Treader; The Silver Chair, and
The Last Battle.

As "space" is the medium of the trilogy, another
common science-fiction element, "dimension," is
that of the children's series. Narnia is a realm visited
at different times by a number of Earth children.
Time in Narnia and time on Earth are disparate, and
Lewis is able to disclose to us within one earthly generation all the centuries of Narnian time from its
creation to the fulfillment of Last Things, the end of
the Narnian world (a joyous, not a sorrowful, culmination).

Dominating the stories is the glowing, golden figure of the Lion, Aslan. (The lion is an ancient but
now little-known Christ symbol in Christian art.)
He is a real lion but he is also the Second Person of
the Trinity, just as in the Nicene Creed Christ is
"Very God of very God" who was made man.
Aslan is the One "by whom all things were made"
and by whom Narnian time is drawn to its close.
Lewis shows us that act of creation, Narnia brought
into existence and beauty through the song of Aslan;
we see, too, the end-that-is-a-beginning as He changes
all things, abolishes all evil, and calls His own to Him
in new being. But nothing in the chronicles matches
for audacity of conception and boldness of invention
the analogue of the crucifixion and resurrection.
Aslan surrenders himself to cruel death as a substitute for others, in fulfillment of ancient law. He rises
again to watch over His creation.

Narnia is peopled with bright, memorable figures: Reepicheep, the valiant mouse; Puddleglum, the marshwiggle; dwarfs, giants, satyrs, beavers, and a wealth of other beasts and creatures. The child who reads of Narnia, while having an enchanting adventure, will see human behavior in its full range; and he will learn the Christian concept of his nature and destiny as a creature.

Because my emphasis has been primarily on Lewis's space theology and dimension-hopping to other worlds, I am in danger of slighting somewhat the most recent of his novels. *Till We Have Faces* (1956) is in marked contrast to the other fiction. It has no overt Christian theology but is no less religiously significant than the other stories. Since its narrative is in a classical mythic frame its meaning is so integrated with the myth itself that it must be left in its expression there.

It is a retelling of the Cupid and Psyche myth, set in a barbarian city called Glome, some distance from "the Greeklands." Lewis achieves the difficult feat of introducing a profoundly significant variation into the form of the myth as we have it from Apuleius. He gives it a new dimension without violating its integrity.

In the myth, after Psyche has wedded her mysterious, unseen husband, her sisters visit her splendid palace and are consumed by jealousy. This motivates their prompting her to disobey her husband. Lewis's change is that the splendor of Psyche's palace cannot be seen by mortal eyes. Her sister (only one is a major figure) believes her to be mad and believes herself to be acting out of compassion and concern for the girl's well-being. So we have a case of someone destroying the happiness of another in the persuasion of acting for that person's best interests.

It is this sister, Orual, so ugly that she goes veiled, who is narrator of the story and its real protagonist. A remarkable woman who leads a bitter life and is a wise, constructive ruler of her city, she tells the whole story as an indictment of the gods. When the story seems complete, abruptly Lewis opens another door. Orual is allowed to state her indictment and finds herself indicted by it. The deep ambivalence of her motives is laid bare. Her document closes—with her life—in the tranquillity after turbulence of a true self-knowledge.

As the opening steps in probing this tale we may reflect on the wedding of Psyche (the soul) to the Divine Bridegroom. The wealth and joy of this union are not visible or tangible to worldly eyes. The worldling—jealous and disturbed by a state incomprehensible to him—is quick to demand that it be proved, to challenge it as delusion, to urge the soul to cast it off in the name of reality. Only when we glimpse the ravage of its loss do we begin to realize what was there. Yet this Bridegroom espouses us even if we lack beauty. Each soul—every soul—may be

Psyche—may share this union, without usurpation
—without jealousy. This I think to be a beginning,
but the ramifications are many.

Till We Have Faces is a remarkable and haunting
book—the more notable because of its contrast in
style and materials to a long-practiced and successful
output of fiction in a different vein. Lewis shows in
it that he is not to be type-cast as a storyteller.

C. S. Lewis is an important voice in the great debate: What is the reality of our being and our environment? The doctrine of Creation (that all things
were made by God) and the doctrine of man (as
a free, responsible, guilty, redeemable creature of
God) are high in his concern. This is the source of
the vigor of his work, the cause of the extremes of
acceptance or rejection which he arouses in people—
for Lewis is bitterly attacked by those to whom his
Christian premises are unsympathetic or unreal. Even
within Christian circles he has his foes. Some are
shocked by his imaginative freshness of statement
and count him unorthodox. At another extreme he
is regarded as too orthodox by those who will not
accept the bold, relentless terms in which he sometimes dramatizes the alternatives between which man
must choose.

His war is upon the diminishers of humanity. In
one of his short polemics, *The Abolition of Man*, he
traces and celebrates that great, world-embracing,

humane, enlightened, and religious vision which is common to Platonic, Aristotelian, Stoic, Christian, and Oriental philosophy alike. For brevity he calls it by its Chinese name, the *Tao*. It is against the *Tao*, as much as any creed, that war is waged by those who deny the objective reality of what man calls beauty, truth, morality, honor, justice, love, and belief, demeaning the reality in which we live by claiming that these entities are mere subjective states of mind.

I am grateful to Lewis for some of my richest experiences of mind and heart. Thanks to him, I can remember with his hero, Ransom, "the Malacandrian sky at morning" and those splendid sights of its night sky, the Milky Way "rising like a constellation behind the mountain-tops—a dazzling necklace of lights brilliant as planets, slowly heaving itself up till it fills a fifth of the sky and now leaves a belt of blackness between itself and the horizon," and then, "the true king of night . . . Jupiter rising beyond the Asteroids."

I can remember with him the awesome glimpse of the Great Dance at the conclusion of *Perelandra*—that Great Dance which is the ultimate order and purpose of all created things.

Am I to say these are not real? I count them among the great symbolic visions of ultimate reality which reveal to us that we are more—and are a part of more—than the data of our senses can record.

The Lord of the Hobbits: J. R. R. Tolkien

J. R. R. Tolkien has defined fantasy as "the making or glimpsing of Other-worlds." As such a maker, his own accomplishment is extraordinary. It is embodied in a four-part work introduced by *The Hobbit* and developed through the trilogy called *The Lord of the Rings*.

The other world which he has invented carries us back into untold depths of pre-history to what he calls the Third Age of Middle-earth. It is a time when men have already long existed, have experienced heights and depths of being, and still share the world with other rational creatures of several different orders, with some of whom, in fact, they have inter-bred.

For this world he has created a self-contained geography, with maps, a mythology and balladry, a history in great depth and completeness of organization, stretching back far behind the time-span of his story. He has created several languages and runic alphabets, and within them traced elaborate linguistic interrelationships and pursued many etymologies. The historical frame of his world is filled out with genealogies and what might be called ethnic treatises on his other-than-human species. There are extensive flora and fauna in addition to those already known to us. All these elements are woven through the tale, but so deep is Tolkien's immersion in this world that at the end of the trilogy there are six appendices, totaling 103 pages, elaborately footnoted, dealing with the subjects remarked above. Though the appendices contribute to the persuasive verisimilitude of the tale, they are not necessary for such a purpose. They reflect Tolkien's own intensity of inner experience and total absorption in his act of sub-creation. It is this that makes his spell so great and in turn draws readers with him into these further compilations of data about an imaginary world they are loath to leave.

The four-part structure of the work is analogous to Wagner's Ring cycle of operas. A shorter, relatively childlike wonder tale (*Das Rheingold* and *The Hobbit* respectively) in each case introduces a massive trilogy. It is odd and interesting that a ring of power is central to both stories and lends its name to their titles, and that dragons and a broken sword to be mended by a warrior hero occur in each. But noting these coincidences between the *Ring of the Nibelungs* and *The Lord of the Rings* is as far as comparison should be carried in a discussion which is not concerned with tracing the incidence of familiar mythic motifs. Tolkien's great work is astonishingly underivative in terms of any specific sources or borrowings. To whatever he has drawn, as all must do, from the common cultural heritage of the human race, he has brought something uniquely his own.

Hobbits are Tolkien's authentic contribution to the lore of imaginary species. They are a small folk, manlike in shape and manner, somewhat furred, seldom attaining more than three feet in stature, but well formed. He tells us they are

> an unobtrusive but very ancient people, more numerous formerly than they are today, for they love peace and quiet and good tilled earth . . . They do not and did not understand or like machines much more complicated than a forge-bellows, a water mill, or a hand-loom, though they were skilled with tools. Even in ancient days they were, as a rule, shy of "the Big Folk," as they call us, and now they avoid us with dismay and are becoming hard to find.

Although hobbits belong to the large and mysterious genre of little people, they are a distinct and fresh invention, richly elaborated in all their histories, habits, and generic idiosyncrasies. Sometimes they are called "halflings" by the men of the story, and are already legendary within its frame so that many are astonished to learn that they really exist. They inhabit a gentle region of Tolkien's geography called The Shire, which has much the character of the Cotswold country.

The sheer creative feat of bringing a new creature into the realm of fairy story is almost too much for some to accept. Sir Stanley Unwin, Tolkien's publisher, told me that the first negotiations for German publication of *The Hobbit* were broken off abruptly when the publishers wrote that they had searched through all the encyclopedias and found that there was no such thing as a hobbit.

Yet it is part of the meaning of these books that this simple, obscure people should play a central role in a great contest involving the welfare of all earth. And it is not that people as a group, but a few individuals from among them, who play the determining role, thrust irresistibly from their wonted quiet into the heart of a vast struggle.

In *The Hobbit*, Bilbo Baggins is inveigled into an expedition by some dwarfs who seek stratagems to destroy a dragon who has long usurped their halls and treasures. The small size and ability for unobtrusive movement of the hobbit is deemed valuable for reconnaissance. In a memorable episode of the journey, Bilbo acquires a ring which he keeps secret for a long time. It has the power of conferring invisibility, which is all that Bilbo knows about it.

The Hobbit is a story which young children love. It can be read to, or by, them from seven years up. To this extent it may be called a children's book. But like any fine story that may lie within a child's range, it is not limited to children and, indeed, can scarcely be relished with ultimate appreciation by them. The more mature the reader, the more added qualities he can discern in it. Stories written not for their own sake, but "for children," seldom are of enduring merit for children or anyone else.

On the other hand, *The Lord of the Rings* cannot be approached by children as young as those who can cope with *The Hobbit*. It is more difficult in language and concept, and prospective child readers must wait a few years. Yet I know from experience that it can be read aloud to an intelligent nine-year-old with immense involvement and response. But the trilogy is an adult book, on any terms.

Its three parts are: *The Fellowship of the Ring*, *The Two Towers*, and *The Return of the King*. In the trilogy, the nature and significance of Bilbo's ring has been discovered by one of the major figures, Gandalf the Gray, a benevolent wizard. The aged Bilbo has turned over the ring to his nephew, Frodo. It proves to be a long-lost and portentous artifact.

A runic rhyme tells of:

Three Rings for the Elven-kings under the sky,
  Seven for the Dwarf-lords in their halls of stone,
Nine for Mortal Men doomed to die,
  One for the Dark Lord on his dark throne
In the Land of Mordor where the Shadows lie.
  One Ring to rule them all, One Ring to find them,
  One Ring to bring them all and in the darkness bind
    them
In the Land of Mordor where the Shadows lie.

Bilbo's Ring proves to be the "One Ring to rule them all." It had been wrought in an earlier age, in the land of Mordor, by Sauron the Great, a malevolent being of immense powers, now devoted to absolute evil. In the past history of the world, he has had times of ascendancy and decline. His earlier loss of the Ring forced him into a long withdrawal, during which he has planned a new campaign. He knows that the Ring has been found. Already he has launched his dark, terrible and corrupt forces to recover it. If he succeeds, all earth and its creatures will be brought under his total sway.

It devolves upon Frodo to attempt to dispose of the powerful Ring in the only way by which it can be destroyed. This is to fling it into the Cracks of Doom, into the heart of the volcanic fire of Orodruin, Mount Doom, in the land of Mordor itself, near the tower which is the seat of Sauron's rule. This heroic attempt and its terrible hazards comprise the story of the trilogy.

The tale is spun out in a masterly way. It is plotted with an astonishing prodigality of invention that never fails in the approximate 600,000 words of the whole. Tolkien can evoke hideousness, terror, horror and dreadful suspense, as well as beauty, laughter, nobility and joy. The style is always graceful, often highly eloquent, occasionally lyrical with descriptive passages of much loveliness and color. Tolkien is an adept painter of scenes and evoker of images, who can orchestrate his narrative and descriptive effects with flexibility and variety, from pianissimo to forte, while keeping his themes or motifs tightly interwoven and steadily developing. Also he is a poet of much skill in the special veins appropriate to the work. He creates runic rhymes and bardic songs in a wide range of moods and meters, from comic to heroic to elegiac, in the modes of those that characterize Anglo-Saxon and Scandinavian literature.

The Lord of the Rings is a fairy tale in the highest aspect of its kind—which requires some discussion. *Fairy* is prominent in the long lexicon of words ruined by the nasty vulgarism of our time—at least in the American culture. It is probably irrecoverable for several generations because it has been made a sniggering, derisive synonym for homosexual. This unhappy association with effeminacy clearly came out of a saccharine sentimentality that previously had vulgarized an ancient and noble conception into a sickly-sweet, flutter-winged miniature image that flourished in Victorian times. To be fair, this corruption had earlier roots, and it has since reached its peak of nauseousness in the excruciating cutenesses of Walt Disney. (God forbid that he should lay his sticky hands upon the hobbits!) What, then, was a fairy before this despoiling, and how is he to be restored to his lost stature and quality?

Here Tolkien has done a great rehabilitation, not only in the hobbit books, but in a long essay, "On

Fairy-Stories," originally delivered as a lecture at St. Andrews University, in Scotland, and printed in the memorial volume, *Essays Presented to Charles Williams* (Oxford, 1947). Professor Tolkien deprecates his expertness, but it is the most profound and illuminating discussion of the subject I have ever seen.

"Faërie," in its essence, means "enchantment." As a *place name*, perhaps its best usage, Faërie is the realm or world of enchantment, whether viewed as remote and separate in time and place or superimposed upon our own, for Faërie is wherever and whenever the enchantment is operable, when men have entered or fallen under it. A "fairy" is one of the denizens of that realm, the people of Faërie, the agents of its natural spells, the masters of its enchantments. A better name than fairy for such a being is Elf, and it is so used by Tolkien as it was by Spenser.

In Tolkien's story the Elven peoples are of major importance. It is before the separation of the ways of men and Elves, before the withdrawal (not the end) of the latter. The Elves are of an antiquity greater than man; are uncorrupted, of tall stature and handsome visage, bear themselves with dignity and joy, preserve their ancient tongue and songs, have rich arts and crafts, which men call enchantments. It is the character of their workmanship to "put the thoughts of all that we love into all that we make." They use their powers benevolently; are immortal but not unconquerable. In a few instances they have wedded with men, producing a race of the

Half-elven, still a noble kind though their powers are less and in them immortality is diminished to long living. All this is in Tolkien's canon. Fairy-tale at large has a tradition of bad fairies along with good, but I suspect that in primal origin the relationship is not unlike that of the fallen angels to the good.

It is important to remember that this realm of Faërie encompasses all the natural phenomena and creatures known to us, augmented by much else in plants, animals, and intelligent beings. In Tolkien's world there are not only Elves and men, but hobbits, dwarfs, and some unique creatures, such as Ents, his oldest living species, a kind of walking, talking tree. There are beornings—a sort of were-bear. We also meet an individual figure, unclassifiable other than as some primal nature spirit, Tom Bombadil. The passage about him is one of the most joyously lyrical and contains, too, one of the finest of the work's many poems.

There are wizards, also. The greatest of these, Gandalf, has profound aspects for further discussion. A wizard, as here drawn, is partly an enigma but seems to be in essence a man, but possessed of long life and magical powers. Following the lead of Tolkien, I have avoided the word "magic" in relation to Elves. Not that it may not be used, but that it may confuse a fine distinction. Enchantment is not a technique that Elves use, rather it is the total natural mode of their being and action. The wizard commands magic as an acquired technique and lore, consciously employed for specific effects, good or bad. From ancient times the lore of magic has known both the black magician and the white magician. Merlin was one of the latter, and even the poet Virgil was sometimes considered so.

Tolkien's world also has a variety of malevolent creatures. At the center are demonic powers, greatest of whom is Sauron, who is unmistakably a satanic figure, who might be nothing less than one of the fallen angelic host, and whose very name suggests the serpent. Orcs form the largest category of his mortal servants—goblin creatures of a debased order —but other mysterious powers, demonic or wraith-like, also are deployed under his command.

Here, then, is summarized the basic frame and cast. It seems wise not to attempt anything in the line of detailed synopsis. On this much we can attempt some examination of the story's meaning. In the first place, it is itself, at its face value, rich with inherent meaning, inescapably bonded with the events and characters. This is meaning of a sort that the reader translates into appropriate analogies for his own life, if he is so minded: as in the fact that courage and integrity, seen in any context, are enhancements and encouragements of those qualities wherever we have need of them. Beyond the inherent meaning lies the possibility of allegorical elements, in which there are many implications, subject to argument and disagreement among interpreters.

As to the inherent meaning, we are confronted basically by a raw struggle between good and evil. This contest offers challenge and demands decisions of several kinds. The power of evil is formidable and ruthless. The initial decision, in which many of the characters participate, is whether or not to attempt to resist it at all. So great and discouraging are the odds involved in resistance that the possibility of surrender, terrible as it may be, seems only in degrees more terrible than the fight—unless the deciding element is the moral choice of rejecting evil regardless of consequences.

Before some of the great ones is dangled the old temptation, "If you can't lick 'em, jine 'em." A corrupted wizard seeks to persuade Gandalf:

> A new Power is rising. Against it the old allies and policies will not avail us at all . . . This then is one choice before you, before us. We may join with that Power . . . Its victory is at hand; and there will be rich reward for those that aided it . . . the Wise, such as you and I, may with patience come at last to direct its courses, to control it. We can bide our time . . . deploring maybe evils done by the way, but approving the high and ultimate purpose: Knowledge, Rule, Order . . . There need not be . . . any real change in our designs, only in our means.

Tolkien pursues still further that most ancient and insidious moral dilemma, the problem of ends and means. If Sauron recovers his Ring, his power will be irresistible. The only means of assuring that he can never recover it is the awful one of carrying it right to the heart of his own realm and casting it into the volcanic fire in which it was first forged and that alone can destroy it. Yet an alternative constantly confronts the Fellowship in its resistance to Sauron. The Ring could be used to overthrow him by any one of several persons with advanced mastery of great powers. It is the nature of the Ring to give power according to the stature of its user—petty powers to the unknowing or inconsequential, vast ones to the strong and adept.

But the Ring and its potencies are evil, conditioned by its maker and his motives. It participates in the essence of its maker. At several crucial times the appeal arises: "Let the Ring be your weapon . . . Take it and go forth to victory!" Each time that counsel is rejected, as here in the words of Elrond Half-Elven:

> We cannot use the Ruling Ring . . . Its strength . . . is too great for anyone to wield at will, save only those who have already a great power of their own. But for them it holds an even deadlier peril. The very desire of it corrupts the heart . . . If any of the Wise should with this Ring overthrow the Lord of Mordor, using his own arts, he would then set himself on Sauron's throne, and yet another Dark Lord would appear. And that is another reason why the Ring should be destroyed: as long as it is in the world it will be a danger even to the Wise. For nothing is evil in the beginning. Even Sauron

was not so. I fear to take the Ring to hide it. I will not take the Ring to wield it.

Here we are brought to the classic corrupting quality of power in direct proportion to its approach to the absolute. Yet, of course, it is not simply the power, in itself, that corrupts, but the pride which power may engender, which in turn produces the swift corruption of the power. The primal nature of the sin of Pride, bringing the fall of angels before the seduction and fall of Man, is the wish to usurp the Primal and One source of Power, incorruptible in His nature because He *is* Power and Source and has nothing to usurp, in being All.

The Ring had found its way into the hands of the hobbit Bilbo, who, in his old age, at the advice of the wizard Gandalf, reluctantly entrusts it to Frodo. Upon the back of the younger hobbit descends this monstrous burden. None of the great dare lift it from him. Frodo's first response is that of anyone caught abruptly in a responsibility too great to contemplate. "I wish it need not have happened in my time."

"So do I," said Gandalf, "and so do all who live to see such times. But that is not for them to decide. All we have to decide is what to do with the time that is given us."

Then, further, Frodo protests:

". . . I wish I had never seen the Ring! Why did it come to me? Why was I chosen?"

"Such questions cannot be answered," said Gandalf. "You may be sure that it was not for any merit that others do not possess: not for power or wisdom, at any rate. But you have been chosen and you must therefore use such strength and heart and wits as you have."

The merit of Frodo, then, is not any built-in endowment, but the painfully, gradually ripening fruit of his response to the challenge set before him.

How Frodo fails or succeeds is the burden of the story—and it is not simple. Comparable tests are placed before other characters and are passed or failed in varying degrees, so that, in all, there are few aspects of challenge and response in the area of inexorable moral responsibility that Tolkien does not exemplify for us in this tale.

The next significant aspect involves the ability of the hobbits to cope with the actively malevolent Ring, so dreaded by greater and wiser than they. It is not to be assumed that the Ring does not work upon them, yet some circumstances help to shield them from its powers, at least at the outset. In the episode in *The Hobbit* when Bilbo acquired the Ring, he began his ownership with an act of pity which had an insulating effect. At the beginning of the trilogy he voluntarily gives it up—something which he alone has ever done—though not without a wrench. In turn, Frodo, though subject to corruption like any creature, begins his guardianship of the

Ring unwillingly and without ambition, accepting it as an obligation thrust upon him.

With so heavy odds, against so formidable an adversary, a significant factor provides one hopeful element in the grim web of Sauron's network of agents, tracking down the Ring. In Sauron's very nature, he is incapable of anticipating the policy adopted by his enemies. He cannot conceive that they would voluntarily relinquish the Ring and destroy it, for it would be incompatible with his nature to do so. Thus, the one move that he does not expect is that they would themselves convey it to his very threshold in an ultimate renunciation and destruction of its power.

Yet counterbalancing this small advantage is a demonstration of the fact that creaturely life does not always offer us clear choices of good or evil. Often we must choose between degrees of evil, and we are fortunate when we know that is what we are doing. Frodo, at times, is compelled to use the Ring for its power of invisibility as the immediate alternative to losing all. Yet every time he does so, two bad results are involved: the always baleful influence of the Ring gains perceptibly over Frodo, and Sauron is instantly aware of its use and his mind is able to grope, in a general way, toward its location, like a radio direction-fix. The expedient of employing it thus is doubly harmful each time momentary necessity forces it. In addition, the nearer Frodo gets to his destination, the heavier becomes the physical burden and the greater the influence of the Ring—consequences of its approach to its source. The question of endurance therefore is progressively acute.

At the outset, the Fellowship of the Ring comprises the wizard Gandalf; an Elf, Legolas; a Dwarf, Gimli; two men, Aragorn and Boromir, and four hobbits: Frodo, his servant Sam, and two others called Merry and Pippin. All the non-malevolent rational species thus have a hand, as well as a stake, in the enterprise. The Fellowship is dispersed early. Frodo must make his grim attempt with the aid only of his loyal servant, Sam. In shuttling narrative patterns of the most prolific story-spinning, the others play a variety of necessary roles in the widely dispersed secondary campaign against Sauron's far-ranging forces.

Now we shall shift to another level of meaning. In this story there is no overt theology or religion. There is no mention of God. No one is worshipped. There are no prayers (though there are invocations of great names of virtue). Yet implicit in the conflict between good and evil is a limited eschatology for the Third Age of Middle-earth. A theology contains the narrative rather than being contained by it. Grace is at work abundantly in the story.

In the Judeo-Christian scriptures, God is seen at work in history, taking an initiative, intervening in the affairs of His creatures. Even in the pagan Homeric literature (and in all other primitive literatures) the heroes are seen operating, as in the *Iliad* and the *Odyssey*, with the constant intervention and support of the gods, without which their enterprises and achievements would be impossible.

In Tolkien's Third Age an Ultimate Power is implicit. There is the possibility of Sauron gaining total sway over Middle-earth, but it is clear that there are other realms where his machinations are inoperable. The "Blessed Realm" lies in the mystery of the West, beyond the Sea, and certain characters sail toward it in an image akin to the passing of Arthur to Avalon.

It is a premise of Christian theology that man must cope with certain of his problems with all his own resources. There are things in which it is up to him to succeed or fail. Yet the Will of God, if not completed through one option, will complete itself through another, and in all contingencies there are helps of which a man may avail himself. The Christian rejects utterly the notion that God is dead, or will be mocked, or even that He has withdrawn Himself from human affairs.

In Tolkien's Third Age, the powers that Gandalf and the High Elves can bring to bear against Sauron clearly are derived from the Prime Source, Who is in some way identified with the Blessed Realm. The great ancient names of men and Elves often invoked, are on His side. Running through the story is a thread of prophecy being fulfilled, and Frodo is regarded as "chosen" for his heavy task.

Bilbo's acquiring of the Ring was not just a com-

bination of chance and the power of the Ring itself
to work its way back toward its master. Gandalf
says to Frodo:

> Behind that there was something else at work, be-
> yond any design of the Ring-maker. I can put it no
> plainer than by saying that Bilbo was *meant* to find
> the Ring, and *not* by its maker. In which case you
> also were meant to have it.

A mysterious, over-arching purpose is manifested,
too, in the enigmas of the odd, repulsive, but fascinating creature called Gollum, who had treasured the
Ring for a long time before Bilbo came upon him.
He haunts the Ring through the whole chronicle.
There are moments when he is spared only in re-
membrance of Gandalf's early words:

> . . . he is bound up with the fate of the Ring. My
> heart tells me that he has some part to play yet, for
> good or ill, before the end; and when that comes,
> the pity of Bilbo may rule the fate of many—yours
> not least.

The intricacy of Tolkien's web of cause and
effect, of the interactions of motives and wills, natural and supernatural, is extraordinary and—notwith-
standing the frame of fantasy—profoundly realistic.
As for the choosing of Frodo, it is said:

> This quest may be attempted by the weak with as
> much hope as the strong. Yet such is oft the course
> of deeds that move the wheels of the world: small
> hands do them because they must while the eyes
> of the great are elsewhere.

There is no evading the problem of the Ring:

> . . . they who dwell beyond the Sea would not receive it: for good or ill it belongs to Middle-earth; it is for us who still dwell here to deal with it.

And so it is that the hobbit, Frodo, quietly, reluctantly, in a sustained action surely as brave as any recorded in imaginative literature, assents:

> "I will take the Ring," he said, "though I do not know the way."

Thus, at its core, still leaving unreckoned all the wealth of its detailed unfolding, this wonder tale is rich with teaching for life as *we* lead it. This places it among the true elite of books that can claim to offer such rewards.

Yet so far we have dealt only with inescapable inherent meanings. Possible allegorical elements can be discerned in it, whether or not they were a part of Tolkien's conscious purpose. It is true that things can be got out of a work of art that its creator did not knowingly put in. Yet rather than say it *is* an allegory, which is too rigid for so large, free and flexible a story, I will say that it has allegorical possibilities and suggestions underlying the face value of the narrative. It is some of these which suggest themselves to me that I put forward, rather than any complete and systematic scheme.

It has for me an allegorical relation to the struggle of Western Christendom against the forces embodied, successively but overlappingly, in Nazism and Communism. The work was conceived and carried forward when the darkest shadow of modern history was cast over the West and, for a crucial part of that time, over England in particular.

Although the notion of the Blessed Realm in the true West is an ancient motif, it is no simple association that also makes the Westernese of Middle-earth —Numenor as he calls it (which suggests land of spirit)—and its men, the hope for justice, peace and order. In the story, men are the inheritors of earth and theirs is the new age coming. The other creatures are withdrawing, having completed their destinies, but a man is king again in the West and the future lies with his kind.

For those to whom Christianity—not any political or economic or military system—is the one possible counterpoise to the Communist doctrine of man, Tolkien's image of the West is a meaningful parable. He shows us a challenge that must be met, or to which surrender is the only other alternative. All the seductions and rationalizations are there, including that of accepting a "wave of the future," or of using power in such ways as to supplant the enemy with nothing better than ourselves corrupted into his own image. Though Tolkien could not have foreseen it, a natural analogy arises between the hydrogen bomb and the Ring of power which by its nature could not be used to achieve anything that could be called good.

In both the Third Age and our world, evil is

never defeated once for all. Even men who fight evil devotedly are not themselves free of its taint:

> Always after a defeat and a respite, the Shadow takes another shape and grows again . . . The evil of Sauron cannot be wholly cured, nor made as if it had not been . . . Other evils there are that may come; for Sauron is himself but a servant or emissary. Yet it is not our part to master all the tides of the world, but to do what is in us for the succor of those years wherein we are set, uprooting the evil in the fields that we know, so that those who live after may have clean earth to till.

If we survive the hydrogen crisis, we will find new technologically pressing moral dilemmas, from genetics to space-colonization. There is never a hiding place, or a time when the perennial but Protean moral dilemma has been solved forever. Though we feel with Frodo, "I wish it need not have happened in my time," we must accept the fact that "The wide world is all about you: you can fence yourselves in, but you cannot forever fence it out." We are faced with what Aragorn, foremost of the men in the story, sternly calls "The doom of choice . . . There are some things that it is better to begin than to refuse, even though the end may be dark."

> "How shall a man judge what to do in such times?"

> "As he ever has judged," said Aragorn. "Good and ill have not changed since yesteryear; nor are they one thing among Elves and Dwarves and another among Men."

So, likewise, one faces with Frodo the necessity that he expresses: "It must often be so, Sam, when things are in danger: some one has to give them up, lose them, so that others may keep them."

The parallels for our world continue:

> . . . in nothing is the power of the Dark Lord more clearly shown than in the estrangement that divides all those who still oppose him.

Part of this divisive power is the force with which everyone sometimes nurses the thought

> that he was offered a choice between a shadow full of fear that lay ahead, and something that he greatly desired: clear before his mind it lay, and to get it he had only to turn aside from the road and leave the Quest and the war against Sauron to others.

We have seen enough to show that it is impossible not to be haunted by parallels between Tolkien's Middle-earth and our here and now. Greater than the samples that are offered is the cumulative effect of the whole tale. It is a moral fable on a scale commensurate with its narrative scope.

Other things remain unremarked. The blight of Mordor, and the damage sustained as far away as The Shire, are images of the blight which the first half-century of the industrial revolution laid upon fair lands, especially England. The sins of the Christian West in that era are directly visited upon the heads

of the generations since, in the warped and frag-
mentary version of the neglected Christian ethic
which, since Marx, has been the ideological appeal of
the adversary.

We have noted already the general harmony of the
elements in this story with Christian theology. It is
clear from the nature and powers of Sauron—not always evil, but become so, and not himself the greatest of his kind—that he is a type of the fallen Angels.
In the era of the making of the twenty Rings of the
runic rhyme, even certain of the sub-angelic High
Elves were for a time deceived by him and, with
biblical and Faustian parallels, ensnared by "their
eagerness for knowledge." We learn that "It is peril-
ous to study too deeply the arts of the Enemy, for
good or for ill."

I shun a too-eager search for supposed Christ-
figures in literature, and excessively elaborate con-
structions in pursuit of them. But it is possible to
say that both Gandalf and Frodo, each in his way,
appear not as Christ equivalents, but as partial antici-
pations of the Christ. With Frodo, quite simply and
movingly, it lies in his vain wish that the cup might
be taken from him, and since it may not, he goes his
long, dolorous way as Ring-bearer—a type of the
Cross-bearer to come. More mystically with Gandalf,
indicative of the operation of an unexpressed Power
behind the events, the wizard undergoes a harrowing
prefiguring of the death, descent into Hell, and rising

again from the dead. Also he experiences something of the temptation in the wilderness in his refusal of the Ring which he has power enough to wield.

Professor Tolkien worked on the whole enterprise for more than fourteen years. He brought to it, apart from his great inventive gifts as what he nicely insists on calling a Sub-creator, a background as an authority on Anglo-Saxon language and literature. He is richly steeped in an enormous lore—but it is not that he has pillaged it for his story. Rather he has so profoundly penetrated the spirit of a genre that he has created a modern work in its mode.

Internal evidence indicates that *The Hobbit* was begun as a complete and self-sufficient tale. Somewhere in the stages of its growth, I believe the vision of the larger projection in the trilogy came upon him, and that the gathering darkness and gloom over the remnants of the West in the Third Age of Middle-earth grew from the darkness and threats looming over Western Christendom in the 1930's when *The Hobbit* was written. The trilogy was produced during and after the years of World War II, a circumstance which seems to support much of what I read into it.

The volumes of the trilogy appeared in 1954 and 1955, and were received with a critical acclaim so great as to carry in it the danger of faddism and an inevitable counter-reaction—a natural hazard of any work unique in its time that kindles a joy by its very freshness. The names of Spenser, Malory, and Ariosto were immediately invoked in the search for comparisons.

Tolkien is not admired by all. Naturally some eight or nine years later, in our succession of glutted publishing seasons, the books are no longer on everyone's tongue. This, together with an apparent total temperamental antipathy, led Philip Toynbee, in an article in the London *Observer* in the late summer of 1961, to make a rashly sweeping assumption.

> There was a time when the Hobbit fantasies of Professor Tolkien were being taken very seriously indeed by a great many distinguished literary figures. Mr. Auden is even reported to have claimed that these books were as good as "War and Peace"; Edwin Muir and many others were almost equally enthusiastic. I had a sense that one side or other must be mad, for it seemed to me that these books were dull, ill-written, whimsical and childish. And for me this had a reassuring outcome, for most of his more ardent supporters were soon beginning to sell out their shares in Professor Tolkien, and today those books have passed into a merciful oblivion.

As a small shareholder, I challenge Mr. Toynbee. His case against the book rests on four adjectives. It is clear that the hobbits are not his cup of tea, and he may rest on the unassailable privilege of personal taste. Still—"dull"? This is a judgment only possible for someone allergic to the basic genre. If you cannot or will not enter its realm then you could not truly encounter its proliferating invention and narrative pace. "Ill-written" is a more strange indictment. I am puzzled as to how he can look upon the writing of our time and say this, unless his basic resistance to the story's content has made him impervious to its expression. "Whimsical" is a more difficult and complex idea. Philip Toynbee gives the word a pejorative tone. But whimsical means so many things, and is in some respects so fitting to this tale that a more concrete bill of particulars needs to be offered. What kind of whimsy? How much of it in the proportions of the work? And what is bad about it? There are occasional touches of whimsicality that might not reach one reader, or might irritate another, but they are swallowed up in the scale and scope of the story. Mr. Toynbee seems to have equated "whimsical" with his final accusing word, "childish." Here he has elected the unfavorable suffix, where I would say "child*like*." The kingdom of wonder, like that of Heaven, is one scarcely to be entered except ye be as a little child. I am afraid that the critic here is too anxious to preserve his adult standing because the work lies within the reach of children and contains elements altogether mistakenly thought by some to be reserved exclusively for them.

Philip Toynbee blinds himself totally to the substance and weight of the profound elements in the story which I have demonstrated here. He might wish to challenge their worth, rejecting the conceptual structure of the work, but he either does not know it is there, or simply chooses to disregard it. Challenge would be a legitimate critical posture—lack of perception is not. His conclusion is, "today those books have passed into a merciful oblivion."

What Toynbee mistakes for oblivion is, instead, a constantly growing following. To continue his own metaphor, those of us who have held on to our shares feel them to be gilt-edged securities. The audience is certain to go on expanding, for it consists of enthusiasts, upon whom the work has made a lasting impression, who reread it, lend it, present it, and always publicize it by word of mouth—that greatest of all media for the dissemination of a book. Because this is not happening in Toynbee's own circle, he is unaware of it.

The English edition of Tolkien has been reprinting steadily from 1954 to 1959. The sale of *The Hobbit* is extremely large. *The Lord of the Rings* has sold over 35,000 sets in England alone. It is an expensive set of books, which means that an unusually high percentage of its readership is through libraries. The double advantage it has of being the kind of book that its enthusiasts want their children to know, and that children in general love, gives it a prospect enviable for any book. If it were to go out of print forthwith it would be certain of a long-continuing audience. Sir Stanley Unwin expressed to me the opinion that the hobbit books were more likely to outlast his own time and his son's than anything else he had ever published, in a career that would include many of the foremost literary figures of our day. Tolkien, retired from Oxford, is at work on another saga creation of comparable scale, to be called *The Silmarillion.* Actually begun before *The Lord of the Rings,* it is a vast myth of the Creation and the Fall. It portrays the earlier ages and some of the history out of which *The Lord of the Rings* arises. There are many of us awaiting it eagerly.

I think it safe to say that whatever anyone might hold to be the flaws, idiosyncrasies, or excesses of the hobbit story, this extraordinary imaginative feat in the making of an Other-world, meaningfully related to our own, is likely to be one of the most tenacious works of fiction in this present age of Middle-earth. It gives joy, excitement, a lift of spirits, and it contains the kind of wisdom and insight which, if applied to the world we inhabit, might help our sore-beset race to hang on through the present shadows of modern Mordor into yet another age.

Many dimensions: the images of
Charles Williams

If you can imagine grafting a Dorothy Sayers detective story onto the Apocalypse of St. John, the
resulting fruit might be like a Charles Williams novel.
His seven remarkable tales are transcendental thrill-
ers, supernatural melodramas. In them, immeasurable
powers are loosed, terrifying events follow, and the
characters live, move and have their being in dimensions which sometimes appall, but through which
Williams shows us the full implications of creeds too
much taken for granted in repetition.

Divine Celestials, the living principles of pure orders of being, devastate the English countryside in
manifestations as great beasts, serpents, and pillars of
flame. Through the ancient mystery of the Tarot
cards an uncheckable tempest is set into furious motion. A man is internally torn and consumed as with
fire while trying to exploit the powers latent in the
stone from Solomon's crown, a cube of the First

Matter with the Tetragrammaton at its heart. The past and the present, the dead and the living, occupy superimposed space and time in a single place. The primordial succubus Lilith walks in the world, tempting minds and souls to drown in themselves. Prester John, in modern England, enters the struggle to prevent adepts of black magic from sacrilegiously using forces potential in the Holy Grail. Such are the elements from which these stories are fashioned.

Human character is seen with intense penetration. Immemorial traits and attitudes of fallen man are vividly isolated, defined, and traced to their conclusions in works and fruits. The cold lust to exploit power at the cost of damnation is tracked along its course of self-destruction. The bodily and spiritual death that comes from total self-absorption is contrasted to the sometimes serene, but also sometimes life-consuming self-giving to both man and God. Fashionable attitudes of this century are shown to us as changes rung on the old sin of Pride.

The books that contain this diversity were produced almost as a casual sideline in the context of a busy and prolific life as an editor at Oxford University Press, and as poet, biographer, critic, playwright, essayist, lecturer, and lay theologian. Williams wrote the novels, as he did so much of his work, at high speed, in neat, tiny script on assorted papers and notebooks. Each unit was so carefully worked out in his mind before pen touched paper, that revision, even in the intricate plots and complex meanings of the novels, seldom amounted to more than interlinear alterations of words or phrases. This happy blend of creative invention with concentration was so controlled that his colleagues often saw him writing furiously, pad on knee, in the inevitable lulls and circular motions of editorial staff meetings. A formidable and extraordinary personality and mind were at work. Yet, "Who is Charles Williams?" could still be the response to follow mention of this remarkable and versatile writer in many literate circles in America, and some even in his native England.

Williams, who died in 1945 at the age of 59, has a hard-core following in both countries which sometimes verges unpleasantly and unsoundly on a cult. Those who knew and loved him best, or who really comprehend the man and his work, would be quickest to reject cultishness. Alice Mary Hadfield, his friend, colleague, and biographer, remarks, "No cult could survive an hour's conversation and laughter with C. W." Apart from the intense devotees, he already commands a broader band of readers which I think is certain to widen steadily. The brief personal memoir by C. S. Lewis that stands as Preface to *Essays Presented to Charles Williams* (Oxford, 1947) is the sharpest, warmest, most touching and charming evocation of his presence and personality.

His major books are all in print in England, and some in the United States. The novels, which are the subject of this essay, have been published in the United States but have lapsed from print here. I think

they will come back. It is of relatively small matter
how soon they do so, for Williams, in his several
modes, is certain to be read for a long time to come.
In all his works he has fresh things to say about ultimate concerns. The persistence of the novels will be
because, as T. S. Eliot has said, "there is nothing else
that is like them or could take their place."

Substantially all of Williams's professional life was
spent at the Oxford University Press in Amen House,
London, until the offices were moved during the
war. For years he worked there at the dullest mechanical aspects of the editorial process, but in time became
an enlivening spirit and powerful intellectual force
in its operations. He was a worldly man in the proper
and profoundest sense of comprehending what this
world is, but was decidedly an unworldly one in the
common usage that suggests the pushing and maneuvering of personal material ambition and the competition for place. He loved the Press, as if astonished
and grateful that it should provide a working frame
for him. He had a rich affection for its head, Sir
Humphrey Milford. Yet in reflection on the whole
history of his relationship with that institution, I
think it a cause for reproach that it did not more
rapidly see the worth of its man, and kept him too
long at work that commonplace men could do. Yet I
think Williams would have rejected such a charge
emphatically.

His earliest writings were primarily poetry. His
themes were the intense inner experiences of the re-

ligious life and of love and marriage. The treatment of human love and the marriage bond as allegories of theological truth was a pattern he pursued from the homely aspects of modern marriage to his famous studies of the allegorical values in the Dante-Beatrice relationship. As Lewis says:

> The belief that the most serious and ecstatic experiences either of human love or of imaginative literature have . . . theological implications, and that they can be healthy and fruitful only if the implications are diligently thought out and severely lived, is the root principle of all his work.

The early poems show the clear signs of the strong individuality of his mind, whatever it touched in any medium. Otherwise they are uneven and primarily of biographical interest. His late poetry, culminating in his Arthurian cycle, *The Region of the Summer Stars* and *Taliessin Through Logres*, is distinguished, difficult, and deep. Lewis considers these "among the two or three most valuable books of verse produced in the century." In the climate of contemporary criticism of poetry it is an understatement to call this a minority opinion. The poetry is a study in its own right and lies outside my present interest.

His diversity of non-fiction includes biographies, criticism, and theological works. Three items from these give him distinction in their kind. *The Descent of the Dove*, possibly his best-known single book, is a history of the Holy Spirit in the Church; a work historically and theologically stimulating, with the stamp of the poet in its conception and execution. *The Figure of Beatrice* is a pillar of modern Dante studies. *He Came Down From Heaven* and *The Forgiveness of Sins* (one volume) are theological essays expounding some of his preoccupying themes and concepts which also are expressed in the novels. Since his contribution as a poet to the Arthurian tradition is so considerable, I must mention his incomplete, posthumous prose study of Arthur. It is published as *Arthurian Torso*, with a long accompanying piece by C. S. Lewis on all Williams's Arthurian work. There is finally a wealth of miscellaneous essays, which have been gathered and published in a number of volumes. His plays are essentially a part of his poetry.

In the midst of editorial labors and this other prolific outpouring, he produced the seven novels, unique in their nature and qualities among modern fiction. Their inexhaustible narrative invention, swiftness of pace, exotic erudition, intellectual penetration, and theological boldness make them fascinating. Their style is dry, which does not prevent him from unloosing a passion of commitment and powerful evocations of awe. The dialogue is sometimes irritatingly mannered, but is as crisply focused and functional as a playwright's must be. The suspense and intricacy of plot are in the classic mode of the English detective story. You hang upon what is going to happen next, and when it happens it is often appalling, unless your defense is to reject its premises out of hand.

A dearth of significant or consequential content is

a plague of much modern fiction. A loss of the vision of the nature of man that has shaped Western Christendom is characteristic of much more. Williams's seven novels have a weight of content and a clarity of vision of the Christian image of man that lend them their special importance.

He is a wholly committed writer. He interprets all of natural or familiar life, plus all of its other extraordinary and mysterious dimensions, in terms of Christian theology. Often in the novels the Christian Church and faith are specific factors, but sometimes they are not directly mentioned, notably in the two last and most complex of the novels, *Descent into Hell* and *All Hallows' Eve* which, of them all, most profoundly realize his theological conceptions. Williams insisted always, in every channel of his work, upon his communication with the agnostic or the outright unbeliever.

Yet it is the inescapable commitment of the books that alienates some readers automatically. In the summer of 1961, the novelist Henry Green, in a moodily dyspeptic piece in the London *Times*, filled with a delightfully candid loathing for almost all his literary contemporaries, remarked in passing:

> There are no barriers in narrative, except that of the religious novel to the irreligious. I have just been reading Charles Williams, who to me is meaningless.

It is paradoxical, in an age when much literature expressly proclaims the meaninglessness of life, that some should find meaningless the firm assertion that life has meaning. On Mr. Green's premises, an immense proportion of the world's art in all media, from Dante to Fra Angelico to the B-Minor Mass, might be held meaningless. His quarrel is not with Charles Williams but with the whole of Christendom, which is so vigorously and annoyingly alive while so many people go about hopefully repeating that it is dead.

Mr. Green means by his "barrier" that Williams's assumptions about life are alien to him—but then, one would think, so must be the assumptions of Dostoyevsky. In the eyes of some contemporary critics, any assumptions are acceptable for serious consideration except those of Christianity, which are enough to dismiss a book as sub-art or special pleading. The variations on the doctrine of meaninglessness, of course, are not considered special pleading, but are taken for granted as if self-evident in the world we inhabit.

The Dimensions of Being

In his novels, one of Williams's achievements is to restore the sense of the awesome, the other, the holy, in our religious life. He evokes what Rudolf Otto, in *The Idea of the Holy,* calls the numinous, and the *mysterium tremendum.* Much of the thought of this century has been influenced by a so-called scientific rationalism. With it has co-existed a split in the several arts between a narrow social realism on the one hand and the intellectual chaos of Zen, or of abstract expressionism, on the other.

In the same period, one blight on the modern life of the Church has been an acceptance of the ordinariness of things. This led for a while to the neglect of the liturgical aspect of worship, and a disproportionate emphasis on social gospel, on works over faith, and the rise outside the Church of ethical-culture movements as substitutes for religion.

The present liturgical revival in the Church is a counter-current in religious life of far more significance than the reported increases in Church attendance. It has analogues in the channels of literature and art. Williams was an early influence in this restored religious vision. He was determined to remind us of the full implications of Christian creeds and worship. He would not allow them to be denatured and shrunken to a remote mythology and a distillation of ethics. Vast and terrible powers are seen operating in his stories—not somewhere else at some other time, but here and now. He brings all the drama of Heaven and Hell and the driving, operative energies of the universe into commonplace English country scenes or the streets of modern London. His pages present the full-dimensioned actuality of a Faith which, to many, remains only words, forms, or benevolent works. His reminders of the implications of the Creeds could drive some out of the Church as readily as they could draw others into it. This is radical theology, sometimes serene, sometimes touched by fear

and trembling. J. B. Phillips attacked the narrow complacency of some parish life with the cry, "Your God
is too small." The God Whose works are seen in the
novels of Williams is not small.

One of Williams's favorite devices for the recap-
ture of the immensity of the Christian vision of life
and Creation is the use of apocalyptic events, by
which he freshens our awareness that human life is
lived at all times and in all places in a double dimension of the natural and the supernatural. He shows us
that, in every act, we are in contact with more than
the supernatural—the supra-natural—for it involves
not only those aspects of nature that overreach human control or conception, but also Him Who is beyond nature because He created nature. T. S. Eliot
remarked:

> Charles Williams was a man who was always able
> to live in the material and spiritual world at once, a
> man to whom the two worlds are equally real be-
> cause they are one world.

Apocalyptic happenings are part of Williams's narrative stock-in-trade. Yet all his work was finished, as
was his life, just before the potentially apocalyptic
nature of our present era was revealed. It is this
apocalyptic possibility of the nuclear age that has
shattered the nerve of some artists and intellectuals.
The Christian should not view it with hysterical
dread and demoralization, for to him it is subsumed
under a redemptive plan that contains all the possi-

bilities of man's wisdom or folly and in which even the onset of the Last Things is not a dreaded disaster but a consummation.

Williams's message is peculiarly valuable right now, not because he anticipated the details of the nuclear age—which he did not—but because the full Christian vision, as he dramatizes it for us, is adequate for the time—and is the only vision that is so. It is a cliché of journalism to remark that earthquakes, volcanic eruptions, and hurricanes dwarf even the power of hydrogen bombs. By how much more the power and judgment of God overreach man's experiments with the natural law Williams can help us remember— though the Christian should not need reminding. It is possible to contemplate even the bomb and not to be afraid beyond that rational fear that besets us in all mortal storms. Fear of the bomb merged with the fear of God offers the best prospect for our sensible management of the awesome nuclear forces.

Where most fiction gives us only the so-called natural dimension of life, Williams always gives us the two worlds of nature and supernature. The difference is like that between looking at a flat picture and then through a stereopticon. In his depth of vision, he seizes upon several themes or subjects which may dominate a whole book and, in some cases, recur from one to another.

He sees the will of God and the will of Satan clashing in the world, but chiefly operating through the wills, decisions, actions and commitments of men.

Men are on their own as regards decision and commitment, but from either the Divine or the demonic side, power and aid can be invoked by those with the faith, knowledge, will and purpose to call upon it. It is a modern catchphrase that men are creatures of environment. This is acceptable only if, with Williams, we give their environment its full dimensions.

A favorite theme with Williams, as it was with Dostoyevsky, who also sometimes used visionary images to express it, was that philosophies can get out of hand. This is the central lesson learned by Damaris Tighe, an insufferable young bluestocking when we first meet her in *The Place of the Lion*. She is smugly erudite, regarding philosophy as "a subject—her subject," as some people regard religion as a subject.

To Damaris, all the ideas she studies and writes deadly learned pieces about are abstractions. What Williams is pursuing here is not anti-intellectualism (which is the essence of the vogue for Zen), it is the resuscitation of the intellect gasping for the air of sense and solid reality. Damaris plays endlessly with

> the dead pictures of ideas, with names and philosophies, Plato and Pythagoras and Anselm and Abelard, Athens and Alexandria and Paris, not knowing that the living existences to which seers and saints had looked were already in movement to avenge themselves on her . . . Gnostic traditions, medieval rituals, Aeons and Archangels—they were cards she was playing in her own game. But she didn't know, she didn't understand. It wasn't her fault; it was the fault of her time, her culture, her education—the

pseudo-knowledge that affected all the learned, the pseudo-scepticism that infected all the unlearned, in an age of pretence. . . .

The appalling energies that dabblers with eternal principles set loose, force her at last to a grasp of what is operating behind ideas, conceptions, that have become long separated from their referents. It is more dangerous to mistake realities for abstractions than any error that is likely to be made the other way round. The lesson is partly expressed by the rhyme, twisted slightly from a hymn of Abelard's,

> Truth is always in the thing;
> never in the reasoning.

Damaris is not to forswear her mind and her knowledge, but to use them fruitfully. The means of doing that is through the outward-moving substitution and exchange, which we shall explore as one of Williams's chief ideas. She makes herself capable for the first time of meaningful contact with people. For in the extremes of her abstractionism, even people supposedly dear, her father and her lover, had become virtually abstractions, rather than other persons in the exchange of relationships. In the end she is able to act, not only to talk; able to see that her abstractions exist as entities in ways that she did not know.

The mode of this recognition, as Williams treats it in *The Place of the Lion*, is through awareness of a correspondence between prime things, or principles, and images (sometimes variable) through which we may observe them, knowingly or otherwise. So it is with his Angelicals. In his next book, *The Greater Trumps*, the mysterious power of the Tarot cards is due altogether to the correspondence of their images to primal principles which can be invoked through manipulation of the cards.

He makes a brilliantly original contribution to an old cryptic tradition in his treatment of the Tarots. They have fascinated innumerable writers who have tried to take something out of them. Williams instead has brought something to them. Few of his inventions are more stunningly fine than the table of the little golden, dancing figures, the moving center, of which the cards are but illustrations and talismans.

There is magic in their origin and in their effects, but it is not a vulgar magic as he sees it. He chooses to attribute the creation of the golden images—which also are only representations—and their talismanic cards to an adept who had possessed insight into the mysteries of the Created universe. Thus Williams brings the Tarots into what is in fact, though he deliberately chooses not to name it, a Christian symbolism. These are other, and slightly more profane, images of those same principles, Angelicals, Celestials of *The Place of the Lion*. Like them, if loosed by man they must be redirected again and quelled by man, in free self-offering. And so the mischief of the Tarot manipulators, Aaron and Henry Lee, is checked by the counteractions of Sybil and Nancy Coningsby.

But whereas in one sense I have spoken of the Tarot

images as profane, at the center of them is one treated by Williams as most sacred of all. This is the enigmatic Fool, the one figure on the table of the golden dance that seems, except to the eyes of Sybil, not to move. Its imagery is unmistakable at last when Nancy, interposing herself against the destruction that her lover has loosed, perceives it as that which

> is called the Fool because mankind finds it folly until it is known. It is sovereign or it is nothing, and if it is nothing then man was born dead.

The novel is one of his finest, and it offers two of the most notable figures of women in his work, in Sybil and Nancy. The former has an intuitive and serene sense of the ultimate things and an untroubled readiness for giving; Nancy acquires them gradually by error and pain, making the decision to give under duress.

Power

The lust for power is one of Williams's favorite themes. But since he is dealing in supernatural terms it is supernatural powers that are pursued rather than the ordinary economic, political, or emotional varieties. We see it as the impious attempt to usurp Heavenly powers, the primal sin of pride, the desire to be as God. This is the Faustian delusion: Seek ye first the kingdom of Hell and all the rest shall be added unto you. It involves sacrilege—the abuse of sacred things, the attempt to force the powers that derive from God into purposes that are not God's. This is always visited at last with shattering retribution, for as "He would not suffer His Holy One to see corruption," so He will not suffer His Holy Things to be corrupted. These sacrileges are the really deep perversions, beside which the disorientations of men's sexual adjustments are little matters. Such sacrilege is at the heart of Graham Greene's short story, "The Hint of an Explanation," in which a stranger tries to bribe a young boy to carry away from the Mass a wafer of the consecrated Host and sell it to him.

The impious strivings for power are of several kinds, but in every case its disastrous element is that it willfully refuses to see or recognize the true nature of the forces mischievously invoked. There is in this something of the mythic or fairy-tale catastrophe of Pandora's box, the magical salt mill or porridge pot, and the water buckets of "The Sorcerer's Apprentice."

In *Shadows of Ecstasy*, the first of the novels written but the fifth to be published, Nigel Considine seeks power over death by the application of secrets drawn from primitive African lore. He has prolonged his life for two hundred years by conserving the energies ordinarily expended in shared and outgoing emotional experiences and transmuting them into life energy. He refuses to "waste" himself by looking outward and seeks to draw the world inward. He is striving to lead men toward the power not just to live indefinitely, but to die and resurrect themselves at will. It is this power and an accompanying domination of men's minds that is his central drive, rather than the simultaneous effort to take over the Western governments by revolutionary African risings of which he is master mind.

Gregory Persimmons, in *War in Heaven*, seeks to use the powers latent in the Holy Grail to master the witches' sabbath. His scheme demands the capturing of the soul and body of a child. This is the ancient and obscene sacrilege of the sorcerer, misusing sacred objects and rites in the effort to become an adept at black arts.

Sir Giles Tumulty, who plays a part in *War in Heaven* and a larger one in *Many Dimensions*, is Williams's most callously wicked man. He sees that the jewel of the Tetragrammaton, from Solomon's crown, can be exploited for both economic and political ends. It is the First Matter, from which all things are made, and thus an infinity of things is possible to it. His contemptuous carelessness of the awesome power he holds in his hands leads him thoughtlessly to loose its mystery upon himself, with fearful results.

In *The Place of the Lion* it is Mr. Foster and Miss Wilmot who open the gateway in the screen that separates nature from the great, impersonal Angelicals who are its principles. It is as if the force fields that guard the life of earth were breached, letting the killing radiations of the sun and the rest of the cosmos through to destroy us. Not comprehending the nature of the powers they have invoked, rashly supposing that they can somehow control them and gain dominance through them, they are instead horribly mangled in the passing of the great Images.

Aaron and Henry Lee, in *The Greater Trumps*, are trying to manipulate the Tarot cards to a wrongful end. They are nearly overwhelmed by what they begin, but are spared the retribution in the other books because their offense is not rooted in a comparable malice or defamation of the Holy, and also by the self-offering intervention of others.

In *Descent into Hell*, power is not involved in the same terms as in the earlier books. Yet in it, Lawrence Wentworth subtly corrupts the natural powers of his mind and emotions and commits himself to a self-absorption so total that he is sucked inwardly through his own being into a Hell of his own seeking. The constructive power of substituted love, to be discussed later, is the theme of the book.

All Hallows' Eve returns to the cold powers of sorcery. Simon the Clerk, exercising sway over an enormous following as the Messiah of a false religion, is again supernaturally old through the mastery of cabalistic arts. He seeks domination over the world through control of souls and limited knowledge of the future. He fails and is destroyed through the toils of his own arts. His spells, and all the images he has sent forth, ultimately curve back upon him like a boomerang. He did not know that such evil has a tight and fatal orbit.

Now apart from the particular terms in which all these power quests are presented, their implications apply equally to all prideful abuses of power and to all usurpations or misuse of what is good.

There are necessary human counterforces in each of the stories. No matter how far out of its true arc any of these powerful energies is diverted, it must inevitably snap back. The Order will not be impaired. As it is the agency of men that causes the disruptions, it is men who must help to restore the order. But as even in their wrong manipulation the powers are of God, so in their restoration it is the power of God that restores and the men again are but agents. Yet this agency in harmony and cooperation with God is more important to us even than the grim lesson of the fruits of sacrilege. Sybil realizes, in *The Greater Trumps*, that "Love expected you to do the best you could to solve such questions before leaving It to decide."

In each of the stories, men and women are confronted by the dangerous or devastating operation of forces that other men have loosed and that someone must redirect into their proper channels. What is to be done? The solution, offered in several variations, always lies in offering the Power back to Itself through oneself, by submitting the self freely to the Ultimate Will. In some cases this is done without bodily harm. In others, it involves a freely willed sacrifice.

In *Many Dimensions*, Chloe Burnett's fate has a

superficial parallel to Giles Tumulty's, but from an utterly different motivation and to an equally different eternal result. "The way to the Stone is in the Stone." Chloe's act is to make herself a voluntary path for the Will of God, in respect to the mysterious cube of First Matter. (That cube makes an interesting analogy to Professor George Gamow's speculative walnut-sized package of forces from which the universe may have exploded in the so-called "big-bang" theory of origin.)

What happens to Chloe reminds me of what befell Semele in the myth, when she beheld the unveiled glory of Zeus. Chloe, long possessed by the "dark mystery of being," has reached the End of Desire that is one of the names of the Stone. In speculating on the way to it, her friend and employer, Lord Arglay, has told her:

> . . . certainly the way to any end is in that end itself. For as you cannot know any study but by learning it, or gain any virtue but by practising it, so you cannot be anything but by becoming it.

The immediate downfall of Considine in *Shadows of Ecstasy* is an ironic by-product of the nature of man in one of those whom he is encouraging to become supermen. But in the book, his hypnotic hold upon one person can be broken only at the altar rail by the power invoked and present in the Mass.

In *The Place of the Lion*, Anthony Durrant, "under the protection" (a phrase I borrow from *Many Dimensions*), like Adam, calls the names of the Celestials, as Adam had once named the things of the fresh Creation. In a "litany of invocation and command" he calls them,

> and the Ideas who are the Principles of everlasting creation heard him, the Principles of everlasting creation who are the Cherubim and Seraphim of the Eternal. In their animal manifestations, duly obedient to the single animal who was lord of the animals, they came.

They merge into the pillar of flame and it is as if

> . . . between the sky and earth a fiery sword were shaken, itself "with dreadful faces thronged and fiery arms." The guard that protected earth was set again; the interposition of the Mercy veiled the destroying energies from the weakness of men.

Williams is not sentimental about the powers of Creation, with that persistent and popular sentimentality which comes perilously close to being a heresy in Christianity. He is that subtle phenomenon, the Christian pessimist. His awareness of the dark possibilities of the immediate grows from knowledge of the nature of man and our fallen condition. Optimism, the counterbalance to despair, lies in the expectation of redemption, the making of all things new. Meanwhile, he knows that "The universe is always capable of a worse trick than we suppose."

He makes Anthony uncomfortably aware

> that he existed unhappily between two states of knowledge, between the world around him, the

pleasant ordinary world in which one laughed at or discussed ideas, and a looming unseen world where ideas—or something, something living and terrible, passed on its own business, overthrowing minds, wrecking lives, and scattering destruction as it went.

Williams sees the dread forges of Creation much as Blake saw them in "The Tiger." There is a God of loving-kindness and mercy and bounteous redemption. But the objective powers of His universe are not supportable by human flesh, as witness the lethal radiations of outer space and the fearful tensions that bind the nuclei of atoms. God's forces exist—they *are* —and they will consume flesh that becomes caught in their fields, howsoever. Whether the Stone of Solomon, the Celestials, or the Tarots, it is shown as tragic "to loose upon earth that which does not belong to the earth, or if it does only upon its own conditions and after its own mode." But in Christian understanding, the accidents of the short-spanned flesh are not the ultimate measure of existence, well-being, or salvation.

The Divine Celestials, the Angels, of Williams are not the effeminate images of sentimental religious decoration.

> You're judging them by English pictures. All night-gowns and body and a kind of flacculent sweetness . . . These are Angels—not a bit the same thing. These are the principles of the tiger and the volcano and the flaming suns of space.

This conception probably influenced C. S. Lewis's approach to Angels in his *Out of the Silent Planet* trilogy. His Great Dance in *Perelandra* may owe some debt to Williams's lines in *The Greater Trumps:*

> . . . imagine that everything which exists takes part in the movement of a great dance—everything, the electrons, all growing and decaying things, all that seems alive and all that doesn't seem alive, men and beasts, trees and stones, everything that changes, and there is nothing anywhere that does not change. That change—that's what we know of the immortal dance. . . .

Substituted Love

At the heart of the novels, increasing in clarification, intensifying in focus in the later ones, is a concept toward which all Williams's thought led him. This is his formulation of *substituted love,* which carries with it the related concepts of *coinherence* and *exchange.* I say his "formulation," for he did not invent the concepts. They are the facts of existence and are visible in the Creation, the Fall, the Incarnation, Crucifixion and Resurrection. It was Williams's gift to find dramatic images to heighten our awareness and strengthen our grasp of them. His most matured, concentrated, formal discussions of these ideas occur in *He Came Down From Heaven,* and in two brief, remarkably compact essays, "The Cross" and "The Way of Exchange," both of which are readily accessible in the Oxford Press paperback, *Charles*

Williams: Selected Writings, edited by Anne Ridler.

Coinherence is the mystery of the Trinity ("I am in the Father and He in me"); it is the nature of the Church, visible and invisible, "we in him and he in us" as "very members incorporate in the mystical body of thy Son, which is the blessed company of all faithful people." At lower and sometimes distorted, corrupted levels it is the nature of citizenship that makes the concept of a nation. It is the blood ties of family. It is the coinherence of all generations of men who would not have been born but by the transference of seed from man to woman and the nine-month coinherence in the womb.

One of the major significances of coinherence he sees as the paradoxically intermingled web of good and evil. They are everywhere inseparable, each curiously capable of transmutation to the other in anything that has begun as either one. Man cannot see clearly here, though he tries. God sees it as we do not. Williams does not shrink, or apologize, for God's part in evil as the Creator of all, Who has set free His Creation.

> I form the light and create darkness: I make peace and create evil: I the Lord do all these things.

There are echoes here, and yet it is not quite the same, of the conclusion of George MacDonald's *Phantastes:* "What we call evil, is the only and best shape, which, for the person and his condition at the time, could be assumed by the best good."

This paradox is brought before us implicitly in the novels. It is explicitly explored in *He Came Down From Heaven*. It is deeply related to the words he uses so often, "This also is Thou; neither is this Thou." Everything that is, or happens, derives from His acts; in nothing that is, or happens, have we captured Him. Each of the disastrous usurpations of power is a violation of the coinherence, an attempt to isolate or separate something from it for our use.

Following from coinherence is exchange. Dostoyevsky said, "Everybody is responsible for everybody." Williams says, "We are always in the condition that we are because of others." It is impossible to reflect on that without perceiving the element of responsibility that Dostoyevsky remarked. St. Anthony of Egypt said, "Your life and your death are with your neighbor." In all that is evil and all that is good we are inextricably entangled with others as individuals and in the community. We have variable shares in the crimes and the good works, but however variably, we do share in them. There is a moment in *Shadows of Ecstasy* when Roger Ingram realizes that he is "accepting blood as all men do by living."

Following from these realities is the existing fact and the potential practice of substituted love. This is what the Incarnation is all about. It is the central substitution and exchange. All scriptural exhortations to love one another and bear one another's burdens relate to it (whether before it or after it, for the law of

God did not begin with the Incarnation, though the intention of the law and the intention of the Incarnation are presumably of the same inception).

Lovers, friends, and members of families often practice simple forms of substitution without consciously rationalizing it. These are the natural starting points for applying the principle. To be conscious of it involves dangers, but may also enrich it and increase its effectiveness, and make possible its extension beyond the closer emotional bonds, in true *caritas*. "Let me carry this trouble for you . . . let me take this on—this burden, perplexity, guilt or pain"—these are the motions of substituted love. While Williams has explored the concept in essays, he has dramatized it in the novels. It is present and visible in the first five, but it is the very essence of the last two.

In *Descent into Hell*, that orchestrated superimposing of past and present, natural and supernatural, the poet Stanhope takes on the dread of Pauline Anstruther, who is haunted by a *doppelgänger*. Pauline matures to the ability to practice substitution and learns that it will operate across time and space, life and death. By this she makes herself the substitute for a martyred ancestor, and is herself the source of his cry of dying ecstasy, by which she had long been perplexed in reading of him.

Wentworth, whose is the specific descent into Hell of the title, wills this course obstinately for himself against every proffered aid. Through the knowledge that Pauline gains, the book could well have been called "Ascent into Heaven." The Hell for Wentworth, the very essence of Hell, is the opposite of co-inherence: separation. As observed in "The Way of Exchange,"

> If we insist on it, we can, in His final judgement, *be* separated. That is hell. But only our selves can put us there, and we cannot put others there.

It is noted in *The Place of the Lion* that "being consisted in choice, for only by taking and doing this and not that could being know itself . . . all that was left was to know the choice." In the later book, Wentworth has chosen and stubbornly adhered to Hell.

> He went out of the room, down the soft swift stairs of his mind [a poet's image], into the streets of his mind, to find the phantoms of his mind. He desired Hell.

Man's choice is awaited patiently by God. In *Descent* there is a suicide from one of the story's earlier levels of time. A poor soul, denied the knowledge or opportunity of better choices, he is given the means of knowing the alternatives and renewed opportunities of choosing in his long purgatorial state. But in each step, the universe "accepted the choice; no more preventing him than it prevents a child playing with fire or a fool destroying his love."

It is Stanhope who teaches Pauline the practice of substituted love by offering to carry for her the dread she feels at repeatedly encountering herself, like Zoroaster in his garden, in Shelley's poem. But as another young woman had learned in *The Place of the Lion*, "salvation must be communicated or it would be lost." She is able to help in a small but meaningful way the poor suicide who is working out his destiny in the shadows, timidly moving from the confines of his self-destructive deed. (Significantly, as we will see shortly, he asks her the road to the city.)

In her great substitution, Pauline runs into the mystery of time. In Williams's view, the triple time sense of our finite being is illusion. All things *are happening* in eternity. (We have seen this concept also in Thornton Wilder.) "In the place of the Omnipotence there is neither before nor after; there is only act." Her grandmother, serenely approaching death, answers Pauline's baffled question about the strange gift she has given to the martyr.

> "But how could he take it before I'd given it?" Pauline cried, and Margaret said: "Why do you talk of *before*? If you give, you give to It, and what does It care about *before*?"

The mystery of the *doppelgänger* is resolved in Pauline's free acceptance of the fear suffered by her martyred ancestor. The dread she had long endured was the dread she had lifted from him, so that he might cry out in the midst of flames, "I have seen the salvation of my God." That dread, Stanhope in turn had carried for her before she yet knew how she had come by it. With her understanding and her act of will, Pauline's remembered fear of her image is transformed into joy. It embodies her deepest intention and realization. In flying from it, she had fled from the good because the good terrified her.

> . . . her incapacity for joy had admitted fear, and fear had imposed separation. She knew now that all acts of love are the measure of capacity for joy; its measure and preparation, whether the joy comes or delays.

Stanhope has opened this further insight for her: the possibility of the fear of good. A disciple of Coué keeps reasserting the formula, "Life is good." "Terribly good, perhaps," Stanhope suggests. Later he adds, to Pauline:

> "The substantive, of course, governs the adjective; not the other way round."
> "The substantive?" Pauline asked blankly.
> "Good. It contains terror, not terror good."

With the acceptance of the terror that can be in good —which is what is meant by the fear of God—sentimentality of the heavenly choir, baby angels, and feminized image of Jesus is purged from the religious understanding. Williams himself had experienced the crises of separation and nothingness. Instead of being crushed, he hammered experience into his views of coinherence, substitution and exchange. He was an unsurrendered spirit confronting the terror in the good.

It is the practice of substitution of love in *All Hallows' Eve* that ultimately thwarts the designs of the adept, Simon the Clerk. Betty Wallingford, living, and Lester Furnival (a young woman), dead, both practice it. For Lester, this act becomes the means of progressing from her first shadowy experience of death toward the City, which is another of Williams's major themes.

The City

The vision of the apocalypse, ". . . and I John saw the holy city . . . descending out of heaven from God, having the glory of God . . ." was much in the mind and heart of Williams. The closing chapter of *He Came Down From Heaven* is devoted to it. It is in the image of the City that the preoccupation with the individual soul becomes merged in the community, the vast Church invisible, the communion of saints, the Body of Christ. The tags and remnants of the unfinished, unredeemed entanglements of the soul with other souls and bodies must have been completed, resolved, purged before the time is ready for the entrance into the City.

His concern with the City is seen in much of his work, including the Arthurian poems in which Sarras, the Holy City of the Grail Legend, is its name. But I think it finds nowhere such full expression as in *All Hallows' Eve*, last of the novels, one of the last of all his works, and surely the most extraordinary of Hallowe'en stories. Here Williams, near his own death though no one was aware of it unless he had inward intimations, considers as he had begun to do in *Descent into Hell* eight years earlier, the transition of death and the problems and choices of the dead. In both books, these problems and choices are inextricably interwoven with the living—for a time—and the operation of the substitution of love knows no barriers of time, space, or life or death of the body.

The great progress of the soul is from the shadow environs of the city of man to the Holy precincts of the City of God. Yet this is not a journey in space, but in perception and response; not a removal but a modulation. Williams saw the city of man in all its aspects and loved it. For him, as centuries earlier for John Donne, London was its embodiment as well as a metaphor for a greater City, and he lived nowhere else except during a necessary removal of his editorial work to Oxford during the war years.

In *All Hallows' Eve*, the painter, Jonathan Drayton, has somehow captured in a picture of the city of London, a gleam of the light from the other City. The soul of the young woman, Lester Furnival, is at first confined to the streets of the immediate post-war London to which her preoccupations were so much bound. Through her ability to grow, respond, and practice substitution she is moving at the last to the ultimate City, unlike the self-absorbed, crippled spirit of her friend Evelyn, who has a long course to go. All aspects of the City are coinherent in London.

There around her lay not only London, but all cities
—coincident yet each distinct; or else, in another
mode, lying by each other as the districts of one
city lie . . . In this City lay all London and New
York, Athens and Chicago, Paris and Rome and
Jerusalem; it was that to which they led in the lives
of their citizens. When her time came, she would
know what lay behind the high empty façades of
her early experience of death; it was necessary that
she should first have been compelled to linger
among those façades, for till she had waited there
and till she had known the first grace of a past re-
deemed into love, she could not bear even a passing
glimpse of that civil vitality. For here citizenship
meant relationship and knew it; its citizens lived
new acts or lived the old at will.

It is the place into which Simon impiously sends the
detached spirit of Betty Wallingford, to probe the
future for his own uses. It is the place toward which
the soul of the suicide in *Descent into Hell* is painfully inching its way. It is the place where "all things
were happening at once."

The writing of this novel, and of C. S. Lewis's *The
Great Divorce*, occurred at much the same time,
which was during the wartime Oxford period when
the two men, with J. R. R. Tolkien and others, were
meeting weekly, comparing views, and reading from
work-in-progress. There seems to be a mutual influence visible in *The Great Divorce* and *All Hallows'
Eve*. Each projects, in effect, a contemporary image
of Purgatory, as Dante projected that of the Middle
Ages. For Lewis and Williams, it is a place in which

the soul takes account of itself, and as swiftly or as slowly as it wishes—or never—purges itself of the old dross in the steps, relinquishments, and choices that make it possible to enter into the new being in the City. Herein, as Stanhope had assured Pauline in *Descent*, "our handicaps are all different, and the race is equal. The Pharisee can even catch up the woman with the mites. Those who do not insist on Gomorrah."

The Novels and Their Readers

When speculatively exploring the supernatural dimension proclaimed by Christian faith, Williams must express its realities in images, metaphors, symbols appropriate to our understanding, but yet drawn from his imagination. This is a process of fantasy, of imagining meaningful things that did not and could not happen literally as projected. He shows us images of the workings of God, but not the actual workings. This is relevant to the warning that Lewis puts into the mouth of the spirit of George MacDonald in *The Great Divorce*, cautioning against representing any projected vision of the other life as its literal reality.

It would be foolish to try to discuss the whole scope of Williams's work in one essay. Not even all the ramifications and collateral or secondary themes of the seven novels can be considered here. I have chosen the novels as the best means of approaching him and sampling the breadth of his range of ideas.

The devices he used in them suggest that he thought of them in this way himself. His best poetry requires some expertness of reading, and not everyone will take up theological essays. Thus, for so much of his message, he flung out the net of the fantastic thriller —not wholly as a lure to readers, but because of the appeal and challenge to himself in the infinite flexibility and possibility offered by the great medium of fantastic story. I feel that for him, as with Lewis, the most powerful expression of his theological thought is found in his imaginative rather than his didactic works.

He deliberately adopted the manner of the English detective story, as C. S. Lewis used the mode of science-fiction. The opening line of the first-published of the novels, *War in Heaven*, is:

> The telephone bell was ringing wildly, but without result, since there was no-one in the room but the corpse.

Here, as with most of the others, he opens with an immediate attention-arrester, and proceeds with a pace worthy of Dorothy Sayers, or one of Graham Greene's "entertainments."

At moments his dialogue is irritatingly brittle and mannered, almost a parody of Britishism. This is partly because, as in the detective story, the characterizations are flat. Yet it would be wrong to say simply that his characters are types, with the suggestion of cliché or superficiality. It is rather that he uses characters deliberately to typify the varied attitudes toward life demanded by his themes. His people have a life more of embodied idea than of flesh.

Although the plots are sensational and the pace swift, there is great intellectual demand upon the reader, increasing in the later novels. His narrative, as well as his dialogue, bristles with intellectual stimulation and is lit up by an epigrammatic sparkle. Encyclopedias are called "the slums of the mind." We are told of someone that, "being a modern normally emotional girl she was, quite naturally, an idolater." A magazine shows the division "between those who liked it living and intelligent and those who preferred it dying and scholarly. . . ." Of a bleakly learned young woman: "Peace to her was not a state to be achieved but a supposed necessary condition of her daily work; and peace therefore, as often happens, evaded her continually."

He speaks of "that mingling of utter despair and wild faith which conceals itself behind the sedate appearance of the English." He notes with especial shrewdness a "scepticism forbidding incredulity," for that attitude of mind is almost universally assumed to be a barrier solely to belief. (C. S. Lewis tells that Williams "used to say that if he were rich enough to build a church he would dedicate it to St. Thomas Didymus Sceptic.") All who have gone to the theatre in London will appreciate: "The National Anthem implored Deity on behalf of royalty, and dismissed many incredulous of both."

Williams's novels will never reach a mass audience, but I think they have scarcely tapped the potential readership awaiting them in both duration and number. Their durability lies not only in the uniqueness that T. S. Eliot remarked, but in the enthusiasm of those who are captured by them, which leads to a word-of-mouth evangelizing by his admirers.

The late James Agee called Williams "one of very few contemporary religious writers who moves and interests me to read. . . . He takes the supernatural for granted . . . and has a wonderful gift for conveying, and dramatizing, the 'borderline' states of mind or Being."

Such reality as there may be in Henry Green's "barrier" between religious novels and the irreligious reader will keep many of the latter from Williams. Even though several of the novels make no overt reference to Christ or the Church, his theological vision admits of no watering down into vague, comforting generalizations, soothing emotions, or canting spiritual inspirationalism. A crystal-hard mind is demonstrating the implications of a religion so demanding, as has been remarked of Christianity, that nobody would have made it up. He calls it "the intolerable gospel." The non-believing quester (Williams's skeptic) may explore the novels, and may possibly go away sorrowing because his mind already has great possessions. The forthrightly opposed may read them to arm for war.

The barrier or antipathy felt by some is not just as

Green would have it. There are deeply committed Christians to whom Williams's work is uncongenial or even repellent. As Paul said the gospel was to the Jews, Williams is a scandal to some. This may be due to a shrinking from the unsparing conclusions with which he overrides the comforts of the Faith. It may be due to temperamental unresponsiveness to fantastic literature, by which some are afflicted (a loss dreadful to me in imagination). It may spring from the perplexing personal chemistry of likes and dislikes.

Those who would like to know more about Williams's life and his other work can turn with profit to *An Introduction to Charles Williams*, by A. M. Hadfield (London: Robert Hale, 1959). Mrs. Hadfield's interpretation of the work is the broadest and best presented. Her resources for the portrait of the man are excellent, since she was associated with him at the Oxford Press, as friend and colleague. There is another book-length study, without the biographical dimension, in *The Theology of Romantic Love; A Study in the Writings of Charles Williams*, by Mary McDermott Shideler (New York: Harper, 1962). It is heavy going and muffles the crackling quality of Williams's mind. It comes close to being, in his own words, "dying and scholarly." But it does expound the main lines of his thought in great detail for those who want to approach it that way.

As I have recommended the novels in general as an Introduction to Williams, so I suggest *Many Dimen-*

sions for a first encounter with the novels, and then *War in Heaven*, reversing the actual order in which they were published. From then on, one may go at will, but the chronology happens to be a good sequence, leading us next to *The Place of the Lion* and *The Greater Trumps*. *Shadows of Ecstasy*, first written but fifth published, is the only one at the time of this writing that is difficult to obtain in England. I think it the least successful in conception and devices, though it contains some vivid scenes and sharp epigrammatic observations. Those climactic books, *Descent into Hell* and *All Hallows' Eve*, may be approached first by the hardy, but are apt to have greater impact upon a reader already accustomed to Williams's unique narrative ways and angles of vision. The novels are in a standard edition, from Faber and Faber, London.

If you enter the world of Charles Williams and find yourself one of its citizens, you will retain that citizenship permanently, going often in and out of his borders, for it will take a long time to explore. You will find there a vast conception of both what you are, and where you are.

Index

ABOUT THE AUTHOR

EDMUND FULLER has worked as author, editor, critic and teacher. He has written two novels, *Brothers Divided* and *A Star Pointed North*, as well as diversified non-fiction, including *George Bernard Shaw: Critic of Western Morale*. His reviews and articles appear in *The New York Times Book Review*, *The Saturday Review*, *The American Scholar* and the *Chicago Tribune Magazine of Books*. He has taught comparative literature and the craft of fiction and drama at Columbia University. Mr. Fuller spent last year in England and on the Continent working on a novel, *The Corridor*, to be published in 1963 by Random House. His home is in Kent, Connecticut. He is associated with Kent School.